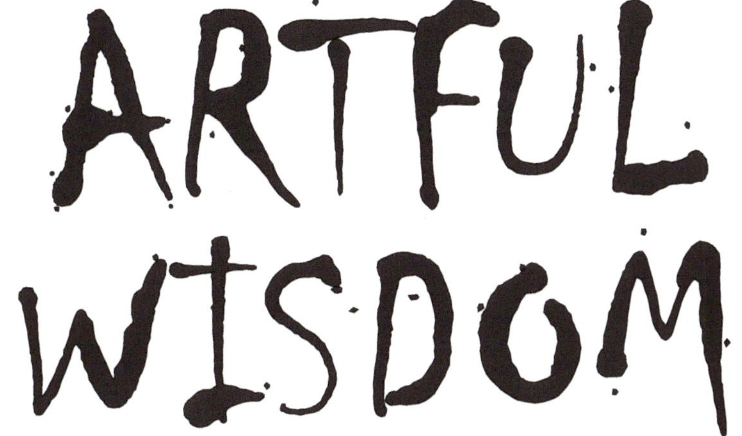

ARTFUL WISDOM

COLORFUL ADVICE

Illustrated by

MARJORY HAWKINS

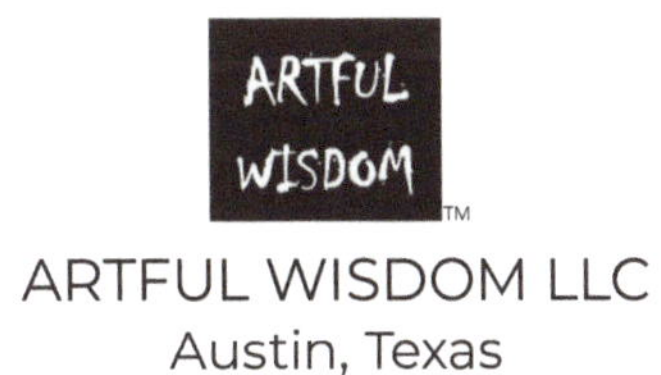

ARTFUL WISDOM LLC
Austin, Texas

Published by

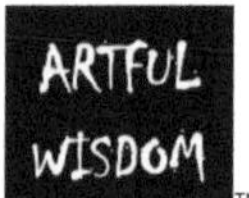

Artful Wisdom LLC
Austin, Texas
www.artful-wisdom.com

Printed in the United States of America

Book Design: Clarity Designworks

ISBN 979-8-9893226-0-2 (hardcover)
ISBN 979-8-9893226-1-9 (paperback)

For Anthony, Vincent, Zoey, Wyatt, Ruby,
and for Jesse, who was the original inspiration

"When a gal's too old to set a bad example,
she hands out good advice."

~ Author Unknown

INTRODUCTION

Unsolicited advice is a dicey thing to dish out. Profound though the advice may be, it is rarely welcomed. But put it in a book and illustrate it with colorful art? Now we're talking.

Originally created as an encouragement for a teenage nephew who detests reading, *Artful Wisdom/ Colorful Advice* is a unique book of art that offers great life advice. The maxims are clever, thought-provoking, and unarguably profound words of wisdom. I wish I could claim them all as my own, but rather, it is a collection of some favorites. I've researched the origins of the quotes and included those I could find; a number of them are anonymous or unknown.

The artwork I can claim, with influences from a wide spectrum. I was first introduced to Outsider Art nearly three decades ago at Creative Growth, in Oakland, California. I fell in love with the colors and simplicity of the art. I became a patron of the gallery and every room in my home features a piece of art from Creative Growth today. I then went on a painting vacation in the South of France, where I was encouraged to let go of all inhibitions around making art. The Outsider artist in me came out and continues to produce.

Hopefully, this art and quotes will resonate as you flip through the book, and they will bring a smile. Maybe they will remind you of a quote you love. If so, please send it to me at marjory@ artful-wisdom.com, and I may include it in a follow-up book and list you in the credits.

Enjoy!

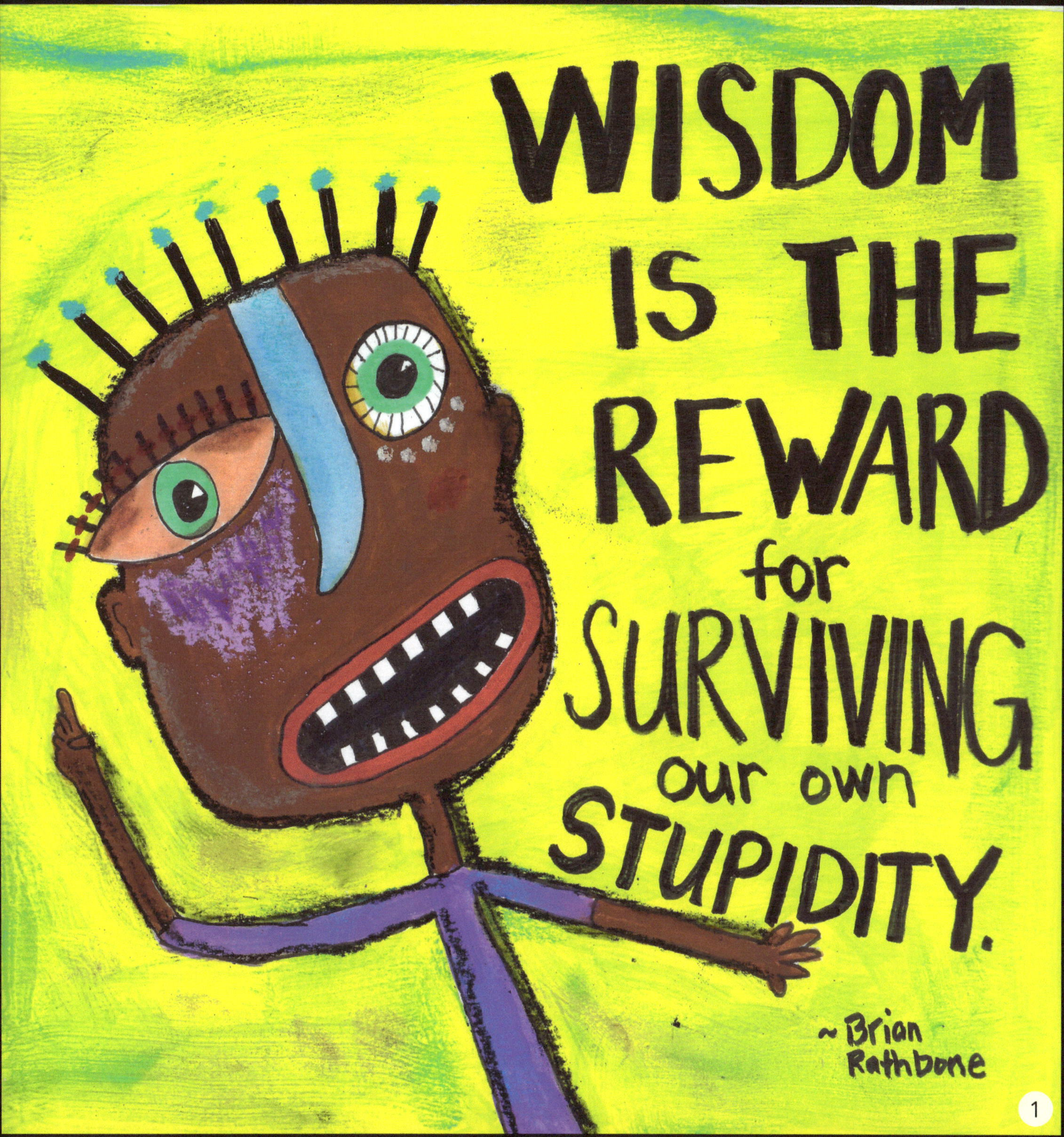

WISDOM IS THE REWARD for SURVIVING our own STUPIDITY.
~Brian Rathbone

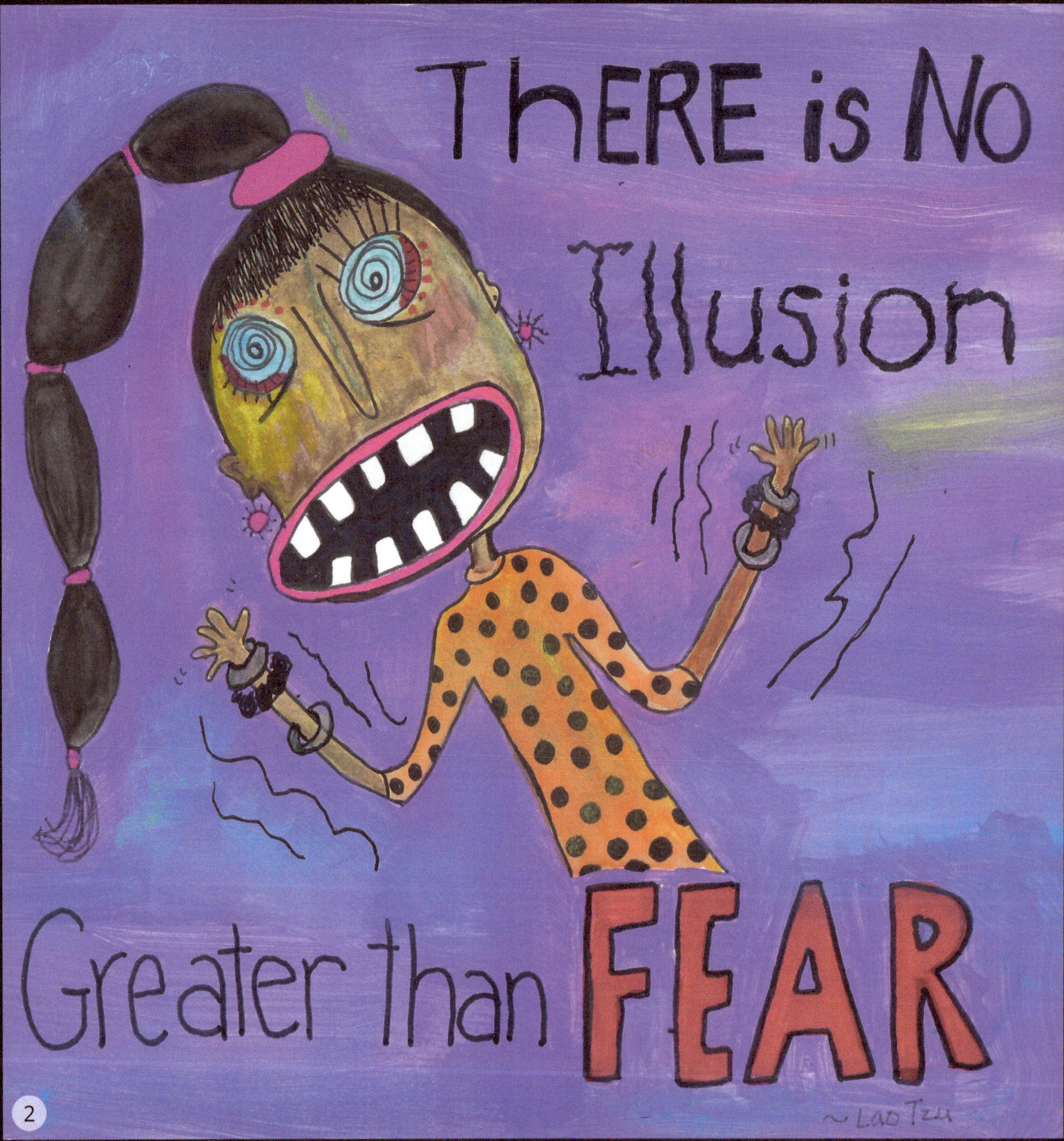

ThERE is No
Illusion
Greater than FEAR
~Lao Tzu

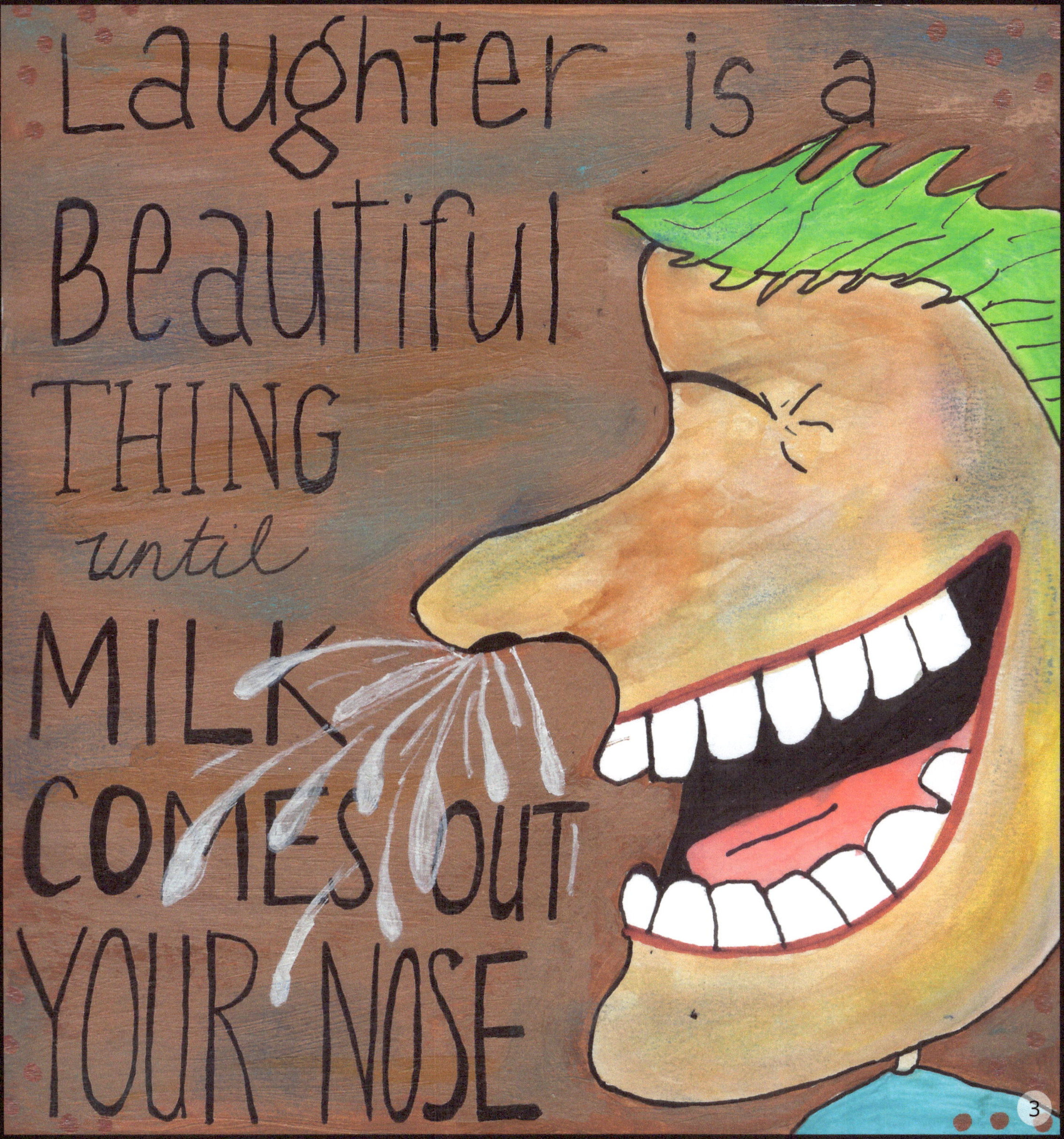

Laughter is a
Beautiful
THING
until
MILK
COMES OUT
YOUR NOSE
3

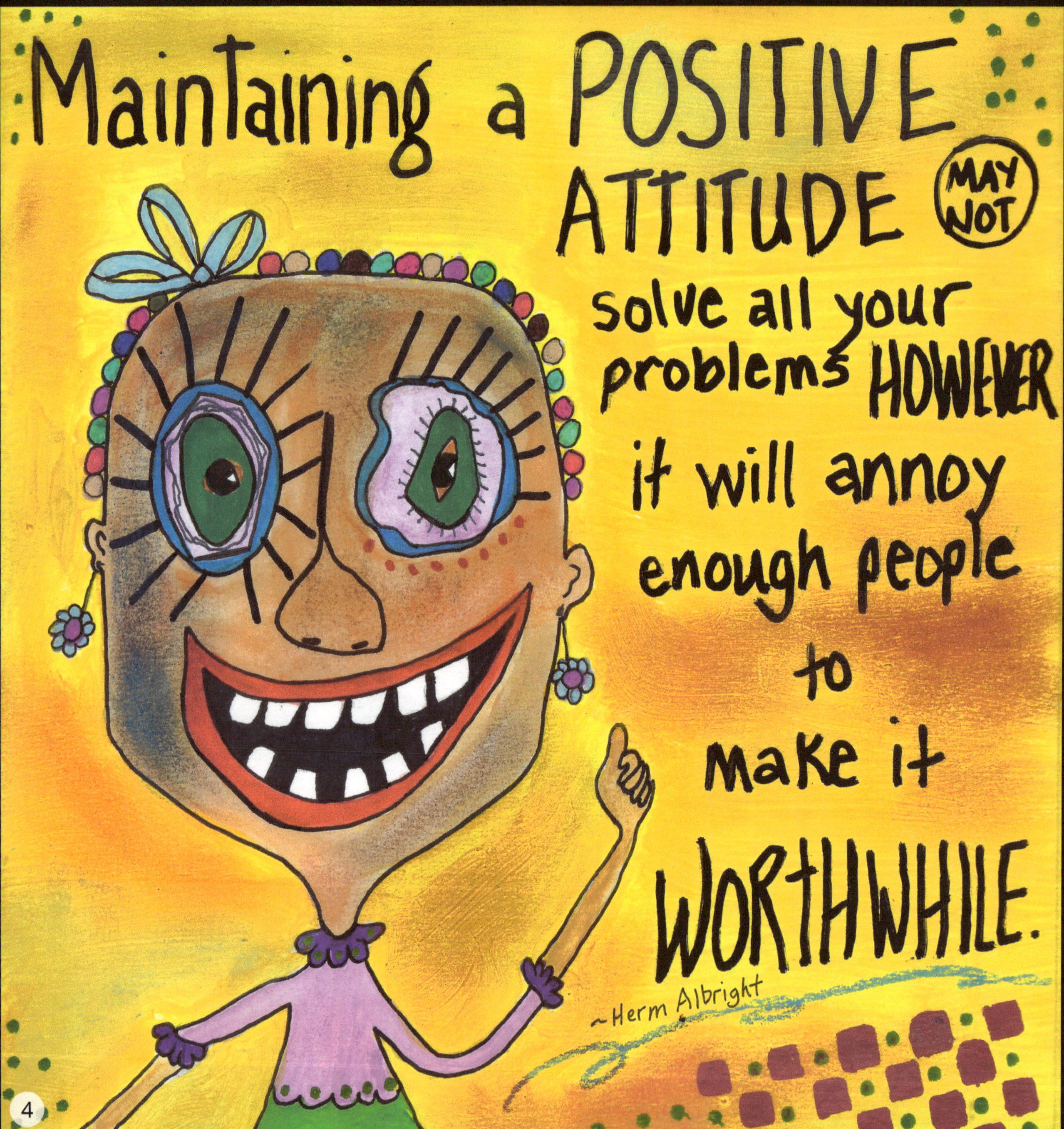

Maintaining a POSITIVE ATTITUDE (MAY NOT) solve all your problems HOWEVER it will annoy enough people to make it WORTHWHILE.
~Herm Albright
4

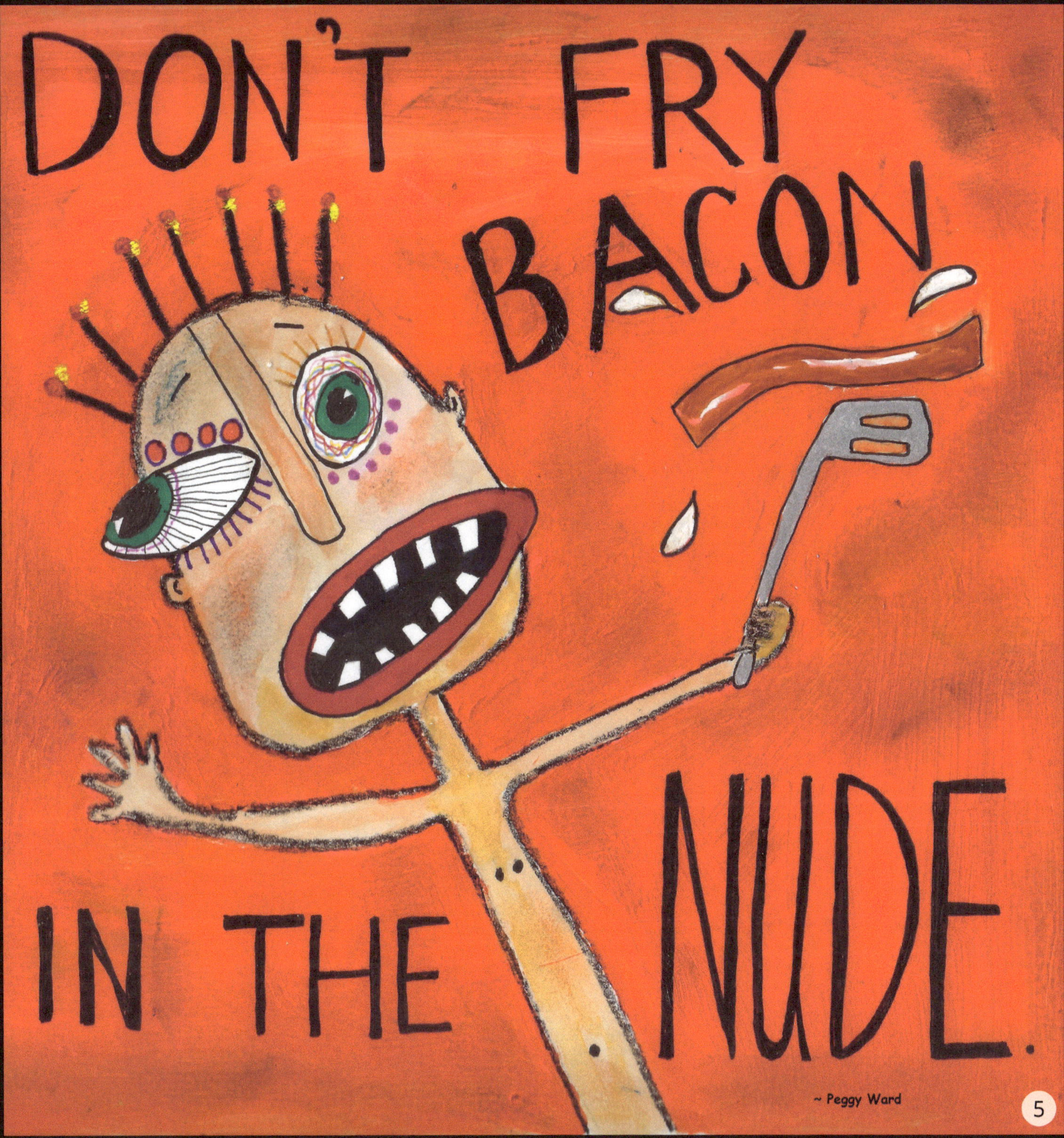

DON'T FRY
BACON.
IN THE NUDE.
~ Peggy Ward
5

If you find yourself in a hole, the first thing to do is to Stop digging!

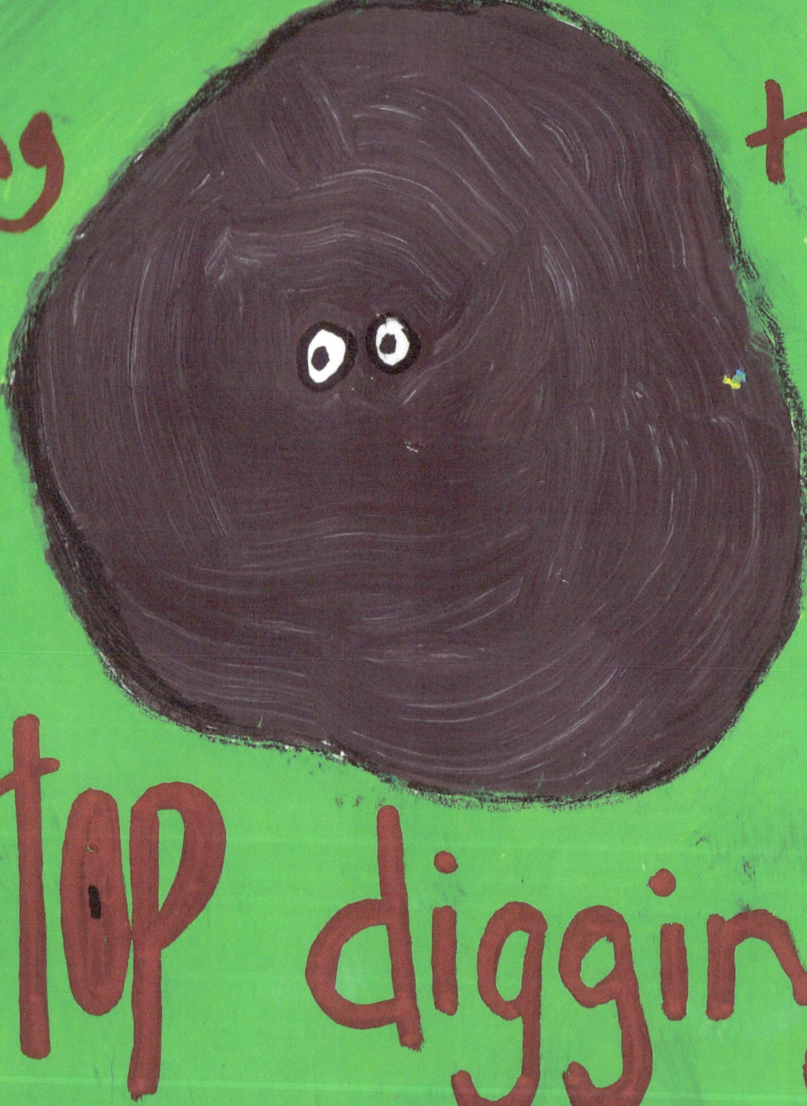

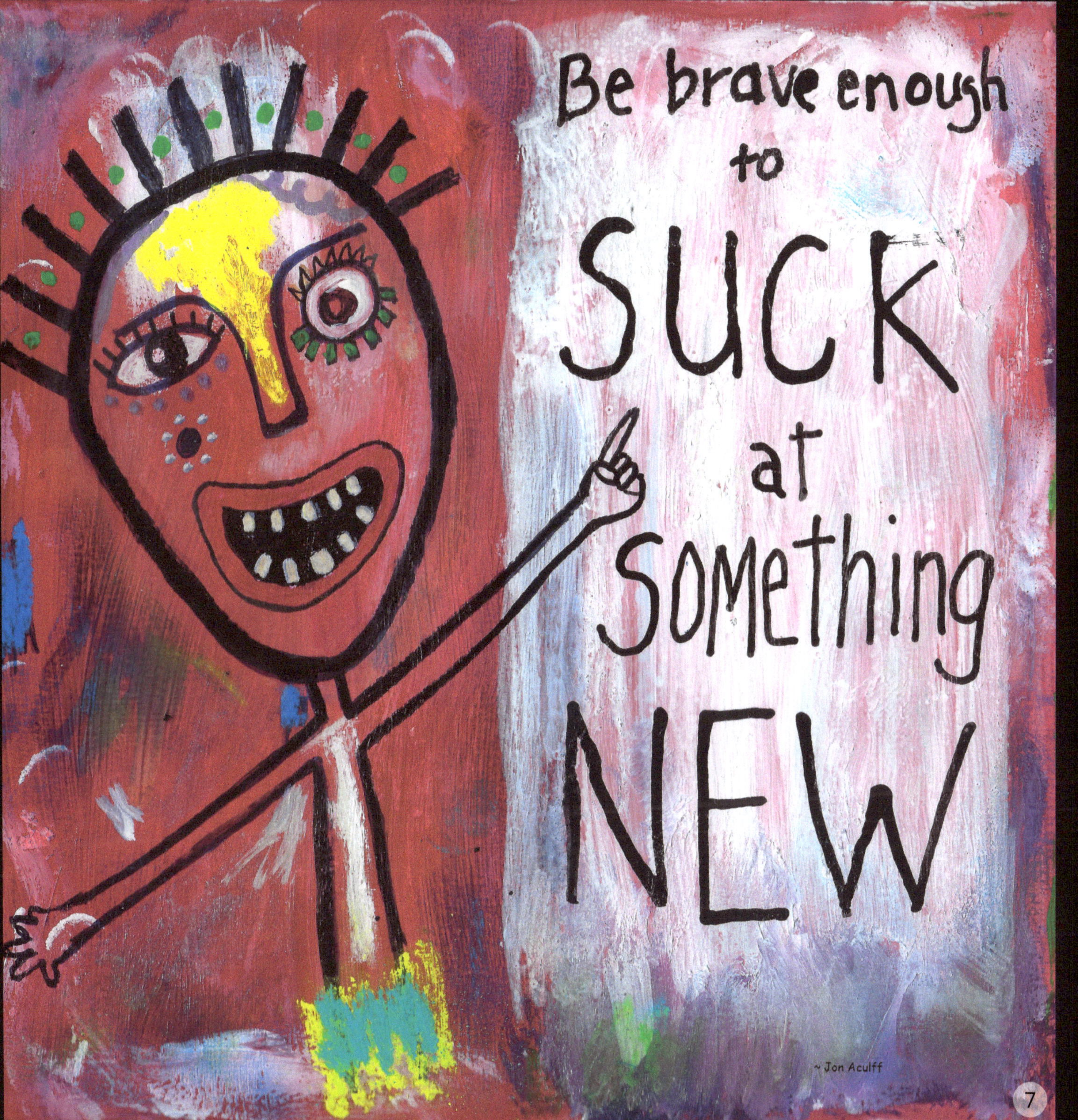

Be brave enough
to
SUCK
at
Something
NEW
~ Jon Acuff

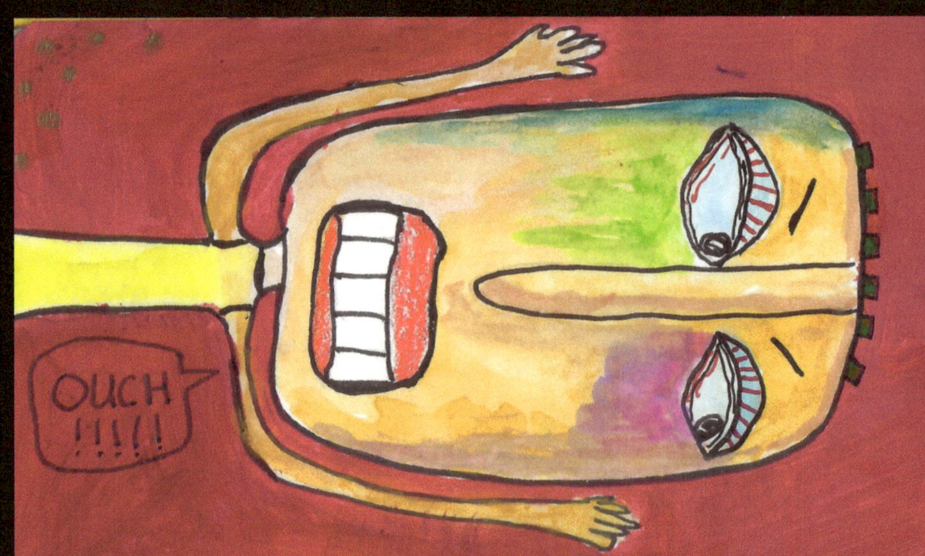

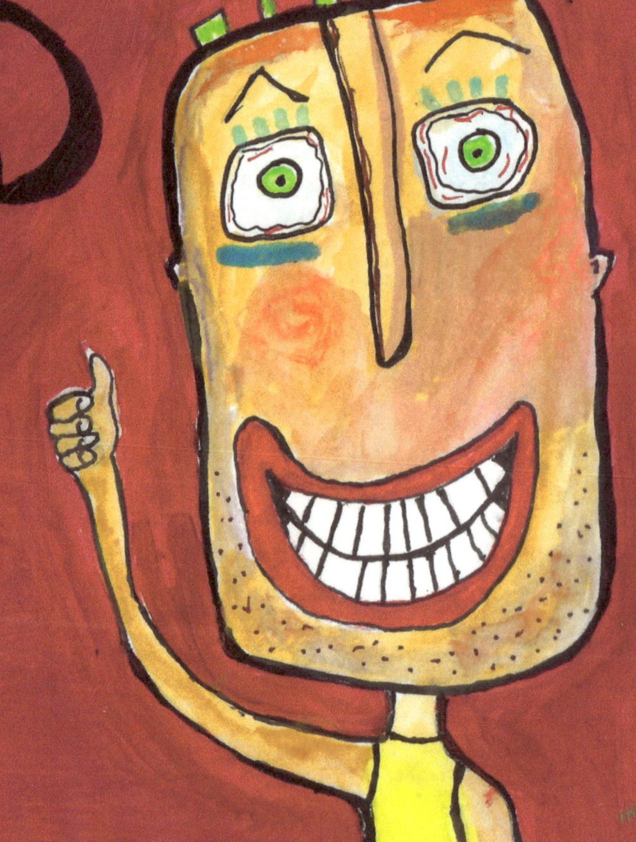

STAND UP 8

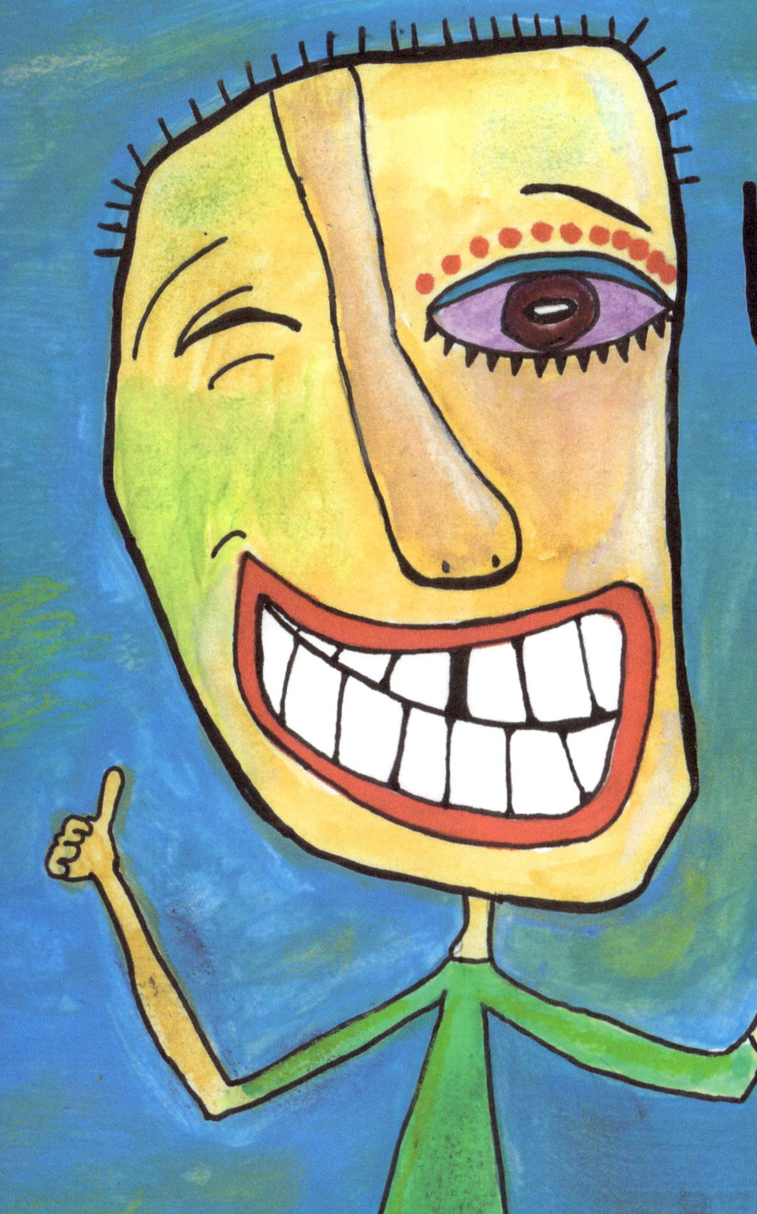
There is Nothing
so
UNCERTAIN
as a
SURE
THING.
~ Scotty Bowman
9

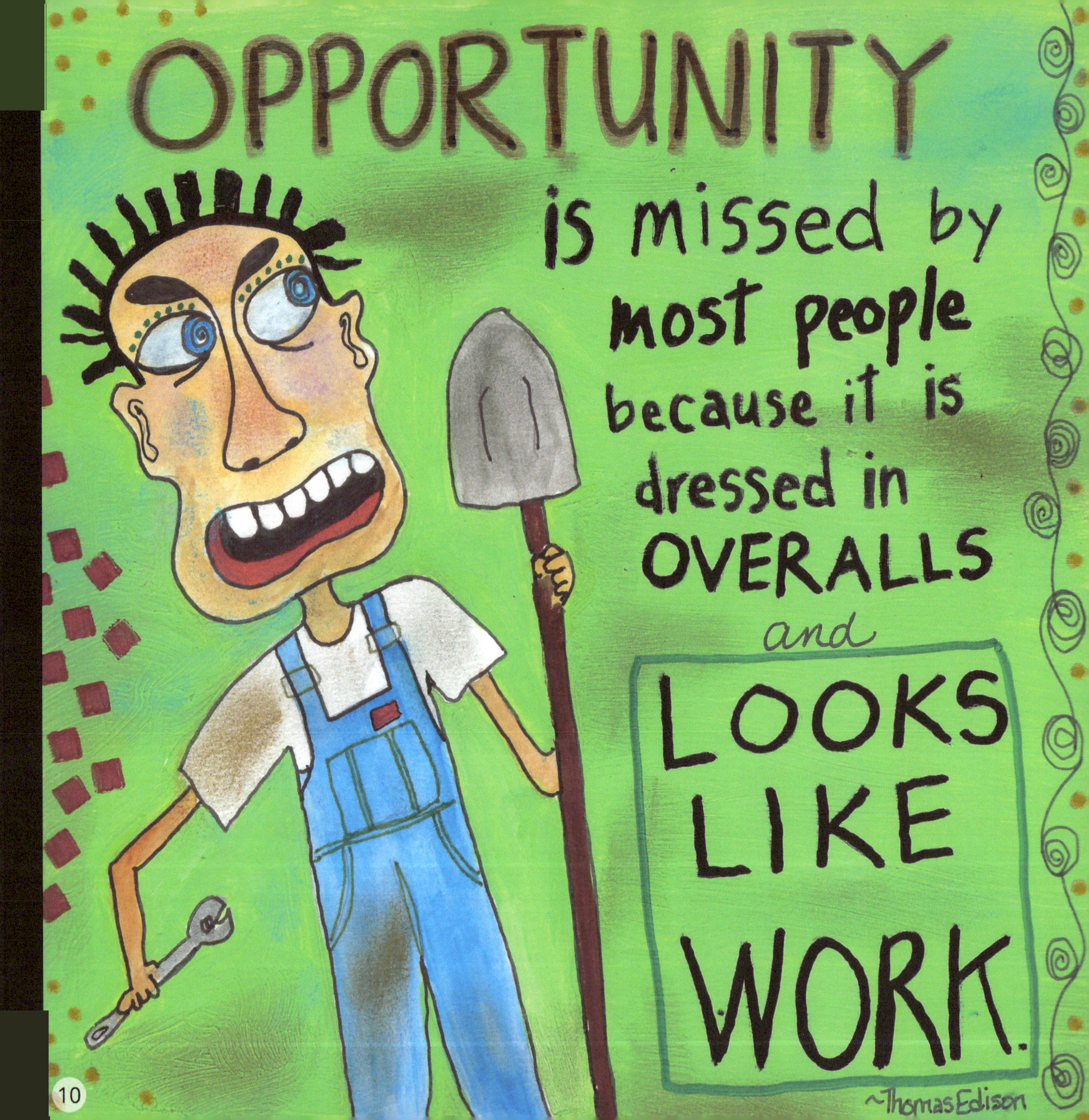

OPPORTUNITY
is missed by most people because it is dressed in OVERALLS and LOOKS LIKE WORK.
~Thomas Edison
10

DON'T SPEND TIME
beating on a
WALL
hoping
to transform it
INTO
A
DOOR. 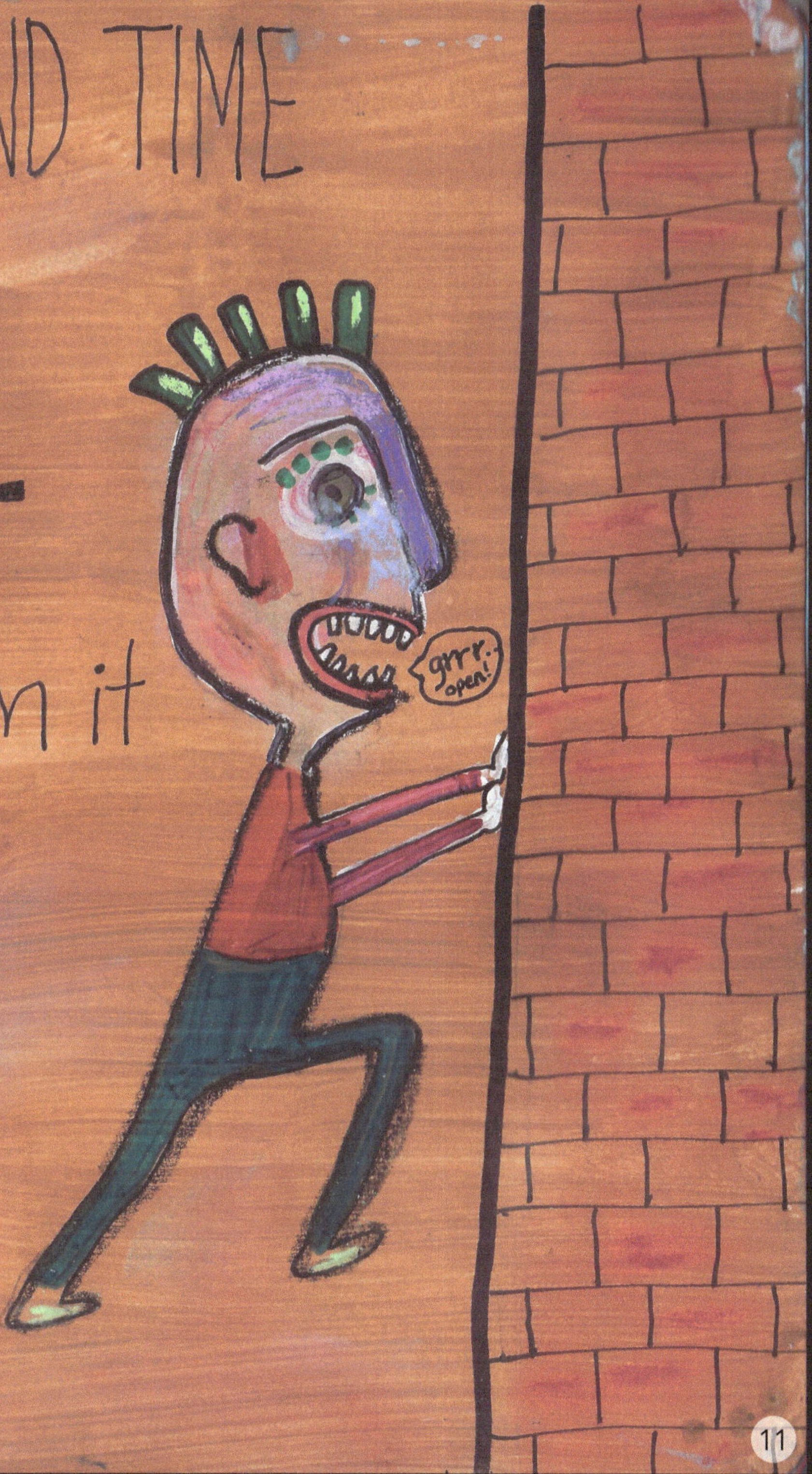
~ Coco Chanel
grrr..
open!
11

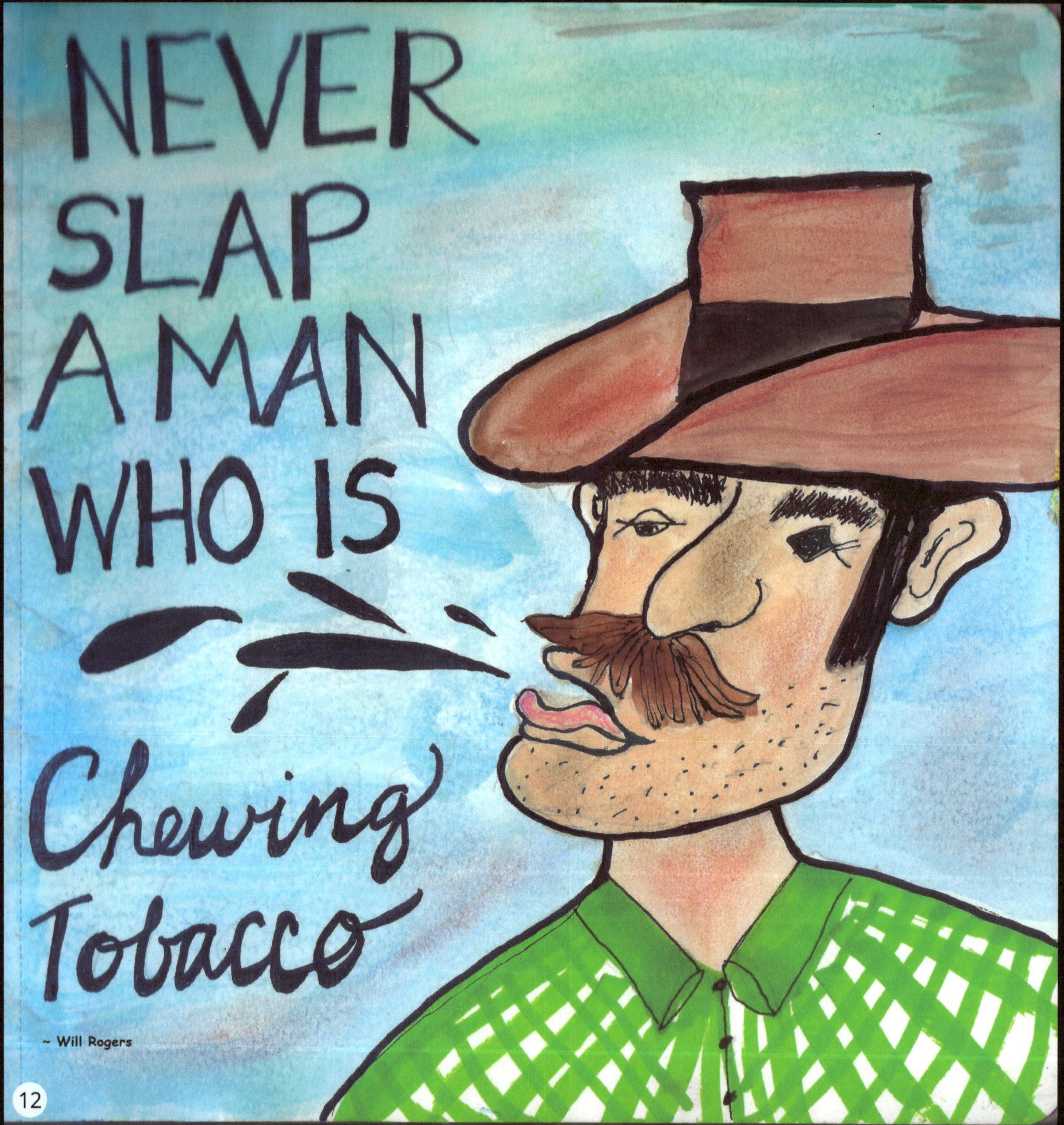

NEVER
SLAP
A MAN
WHO IS
Chewing
Tobacco

~ Will Rogers

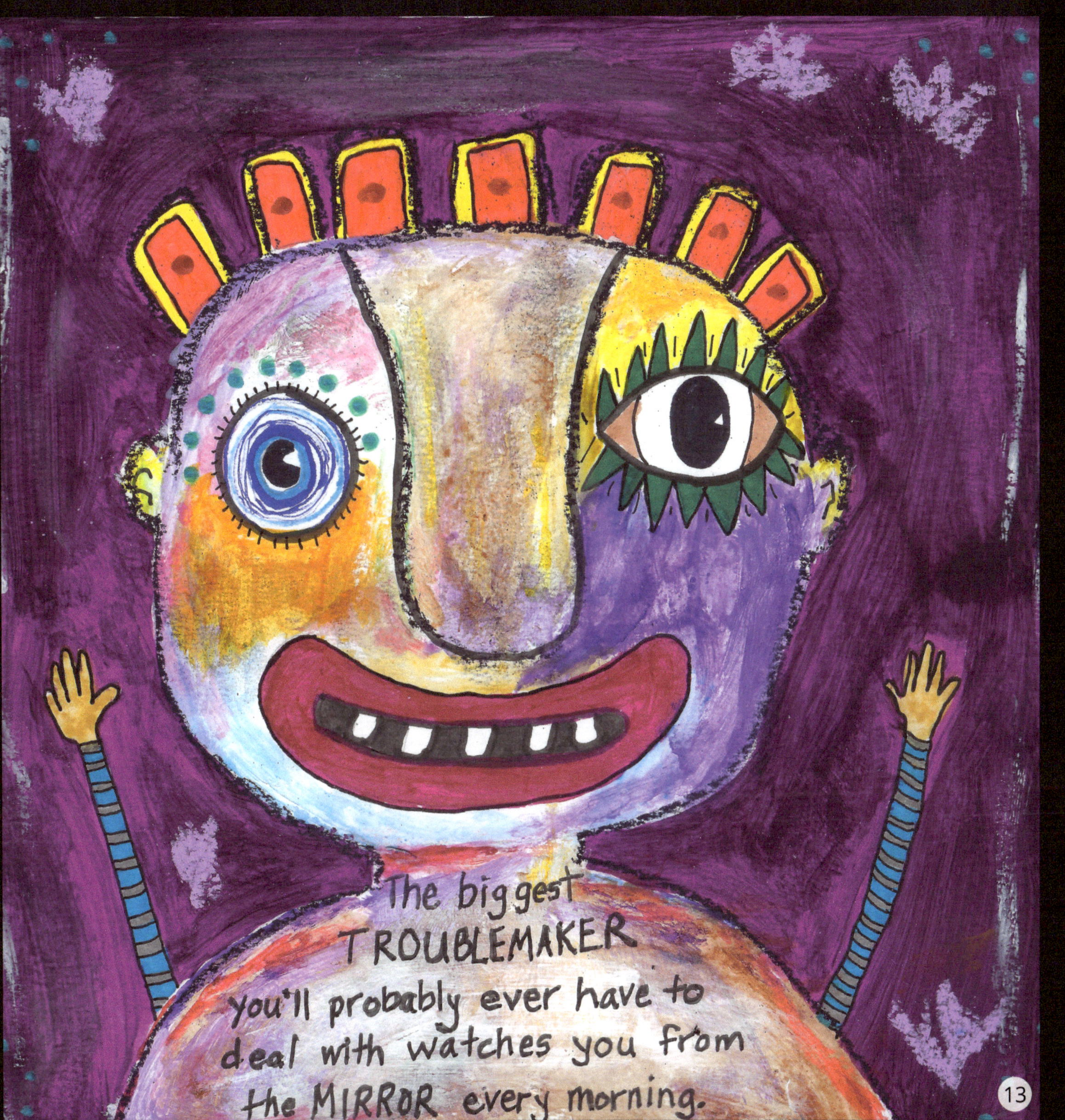
The biggest
TROUBLEMAKER
you'll probably ever have to
deal with watches you from
the MIRROR every morning.

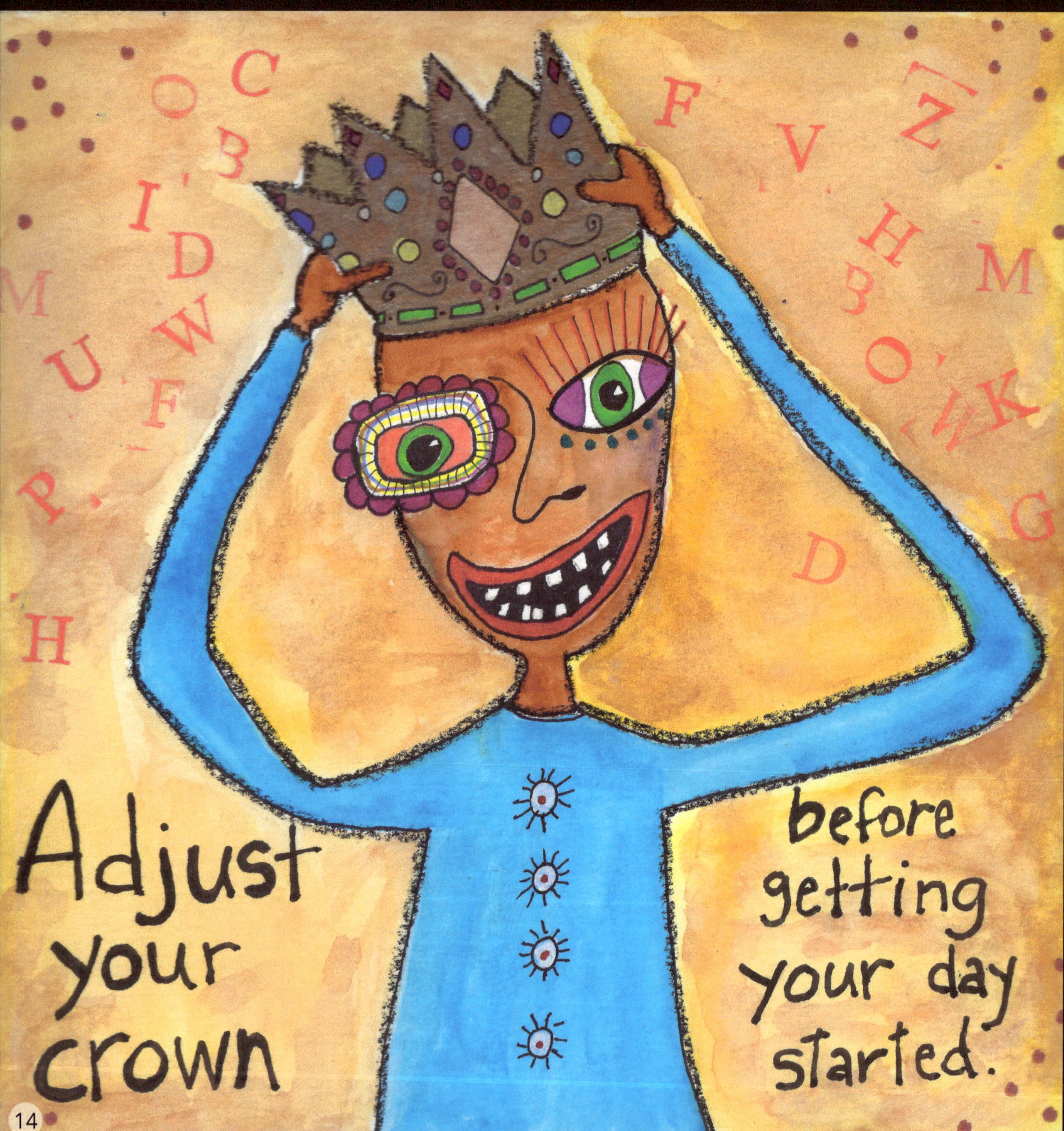

Adjust
your
crown
before
getting
your day
started.
14

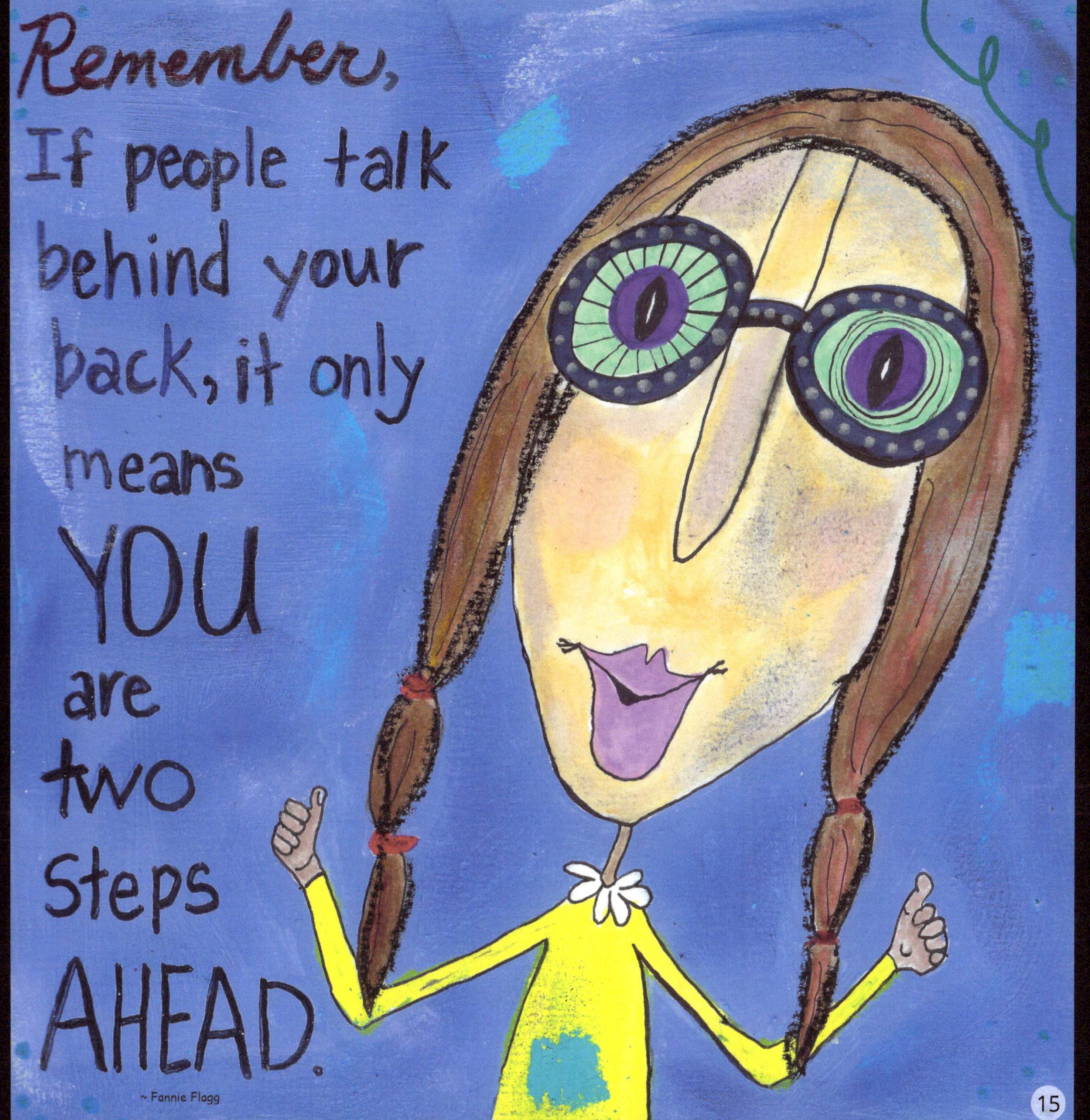

Remember,
If people talk behind your back, it only means YOU are two steps AHEAD.
~ Fannie Flagg
15

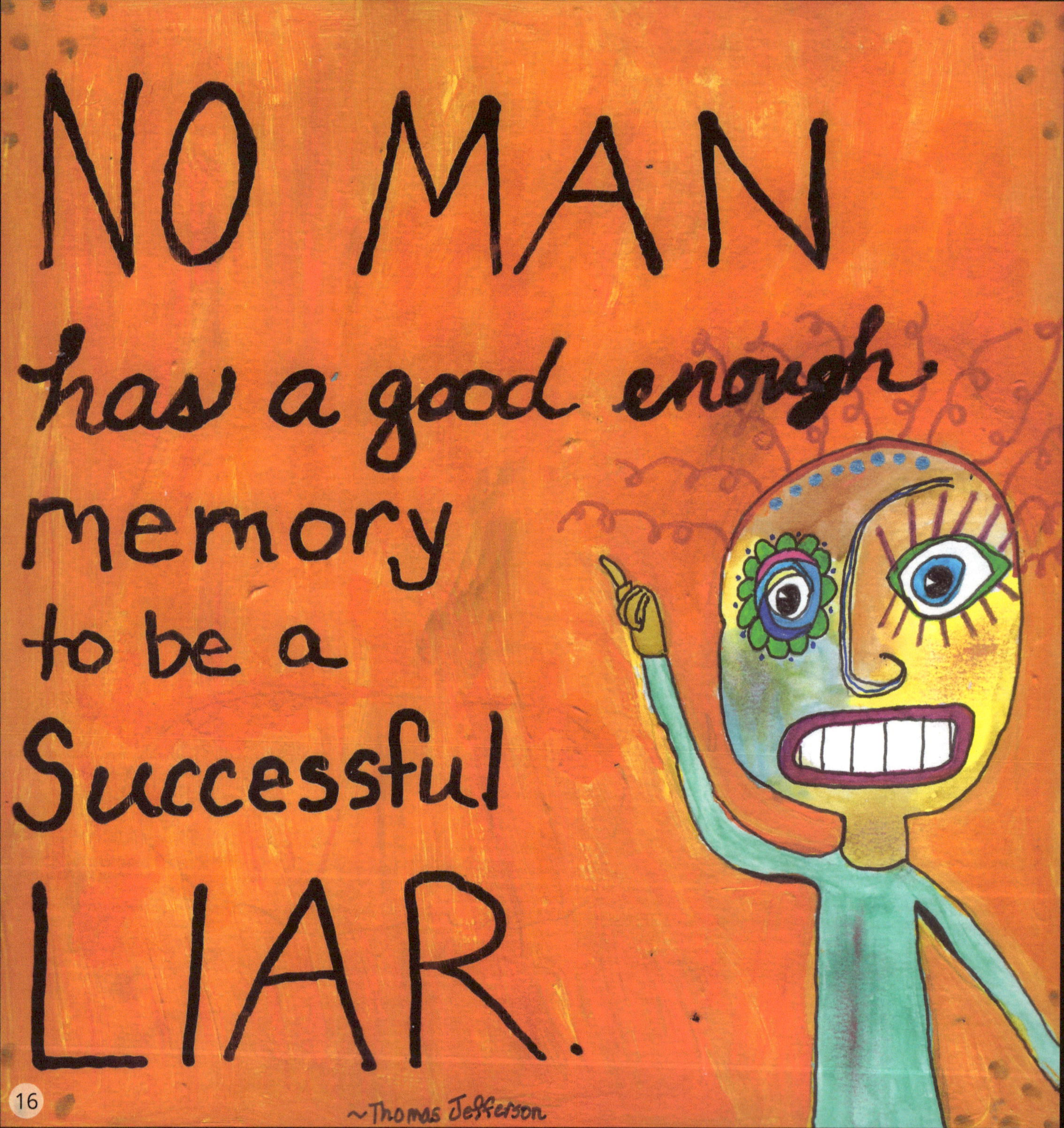

NO MAN
has a good enough
memory
to be a
Successful
LIAR.
~Thomas Jefferson
16

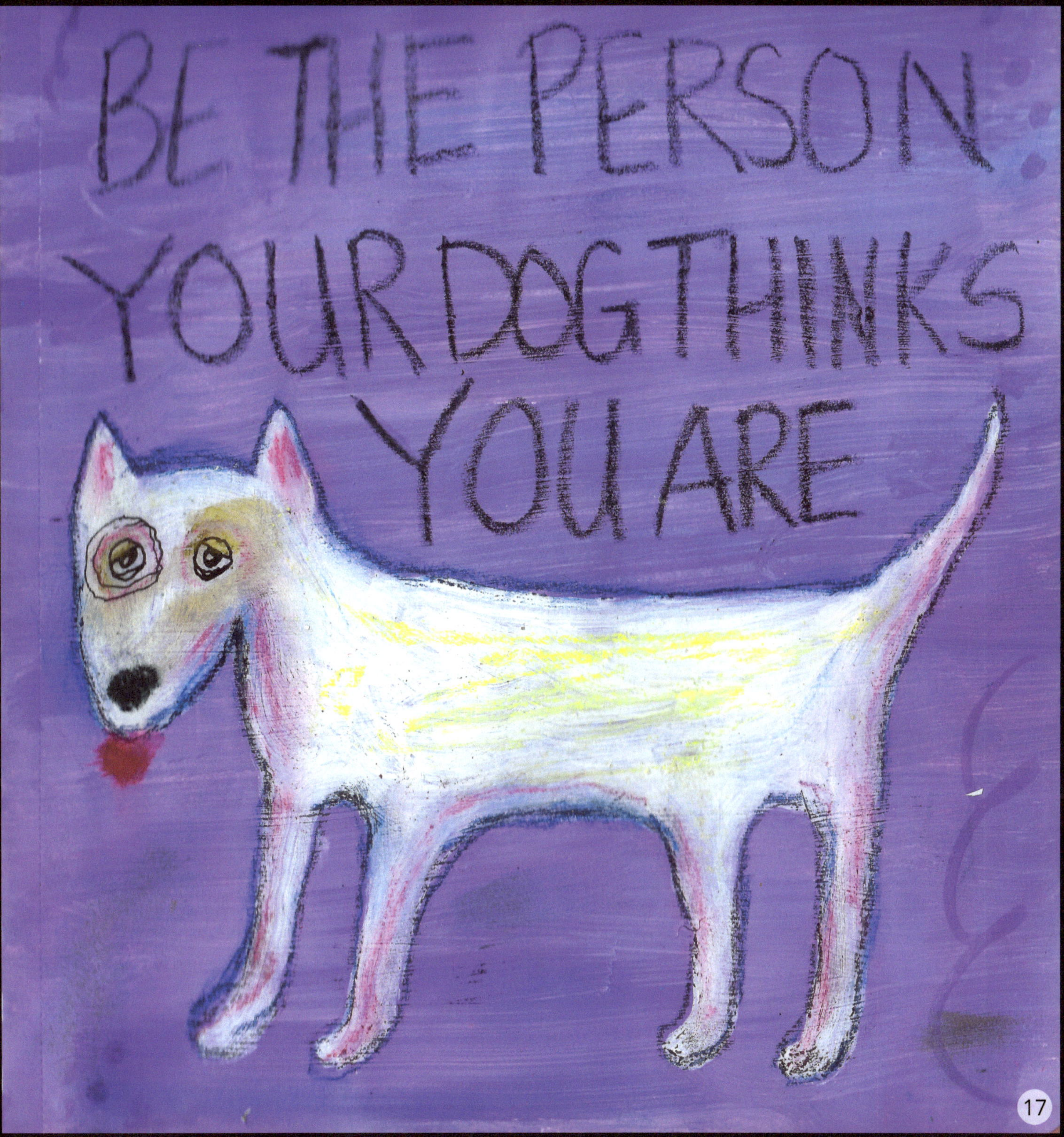

BE THE PERSON
YOUR DOG THINKS
YOU ARE

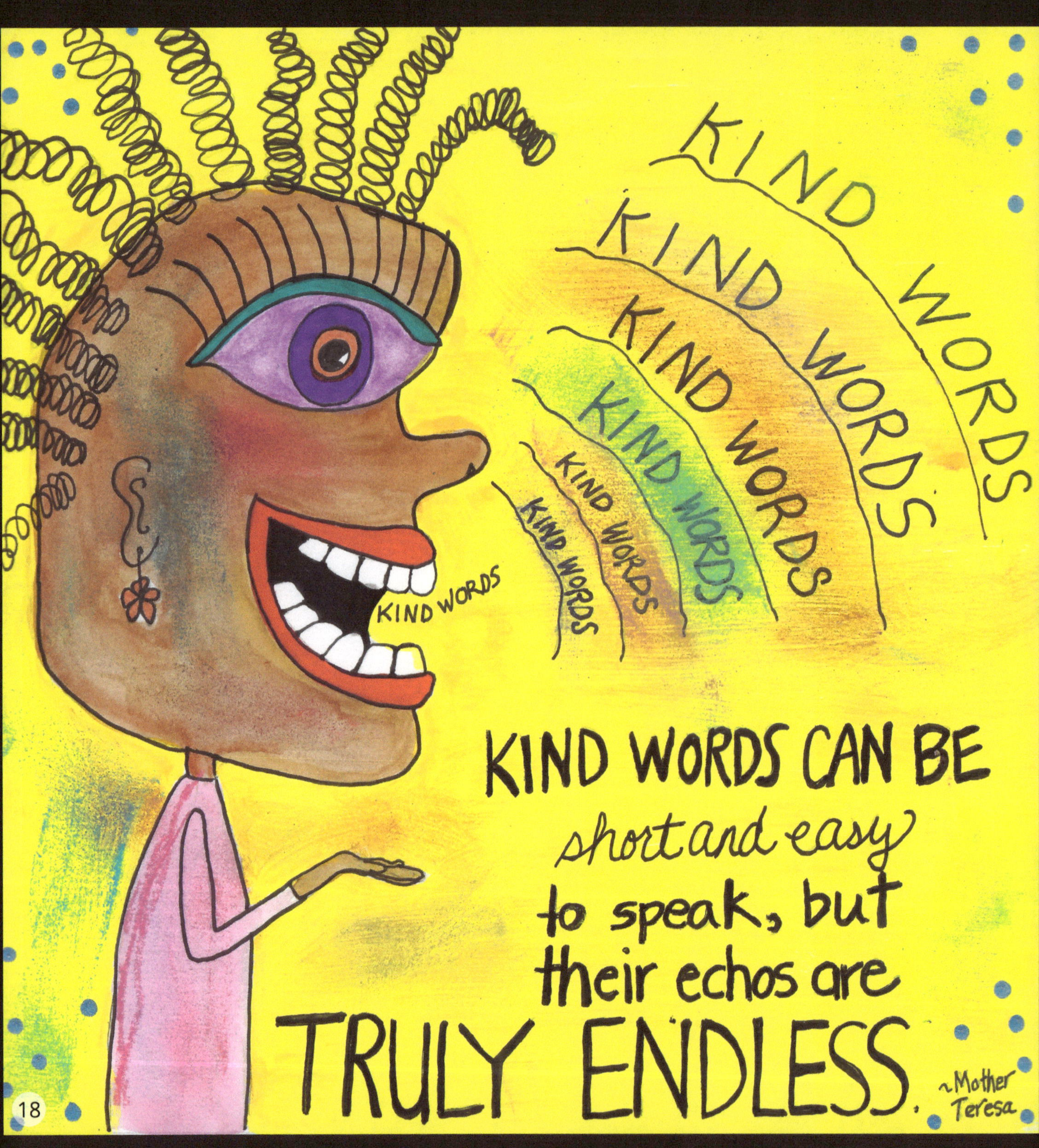

KIND WORDS
KIND WORDS
KIND WORDS
KIND WORDS
KIND WORDS
KIND WORDS
KIND WORDS
KIND WORDS
KIND WORDS CAN BE short and easy to speak, but their echos are TRULY ENDLESS.
~Mother Teresa
18

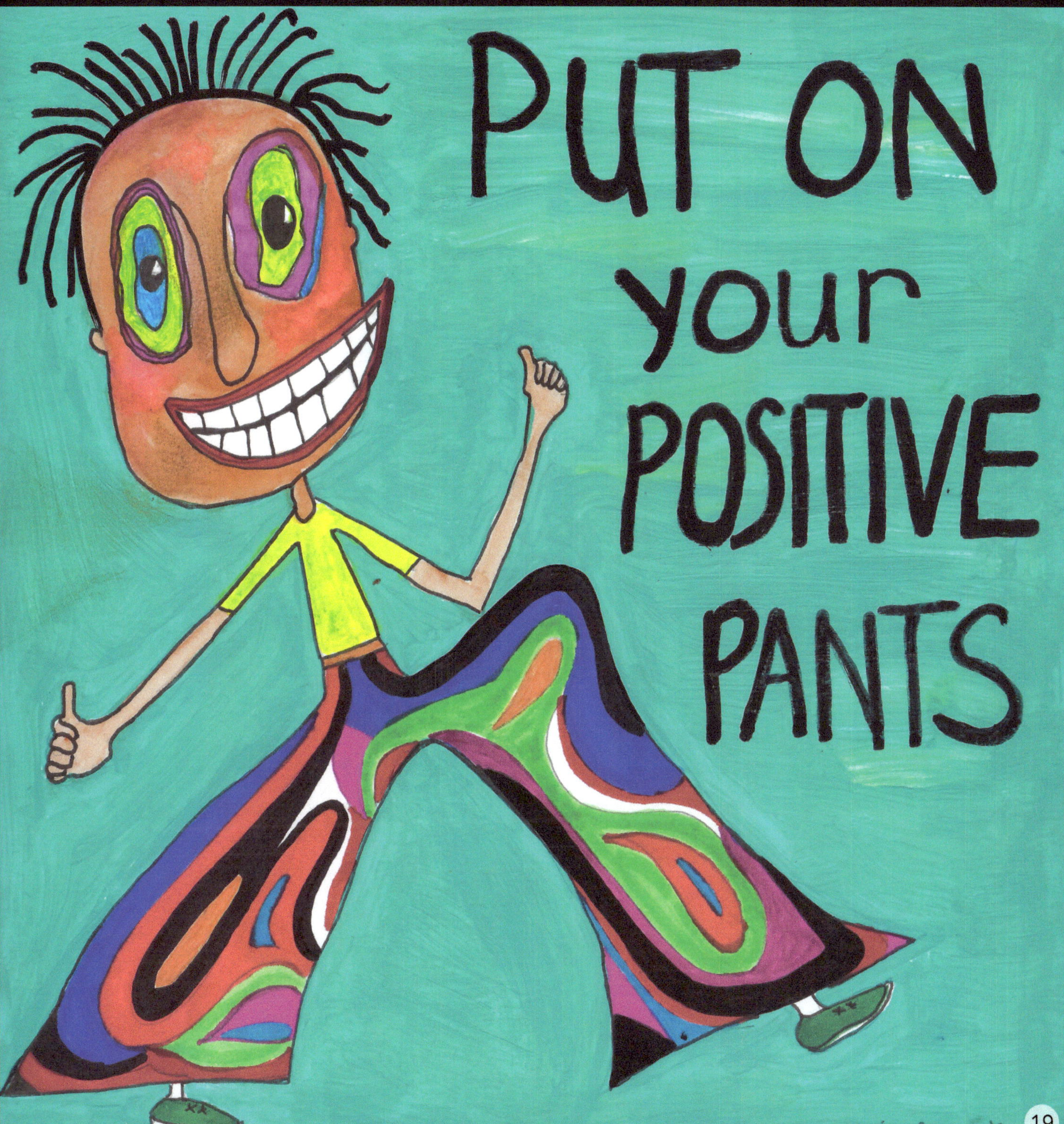

PUT ON
your
POSITIVE
PANTS
~ Claire Clements
19

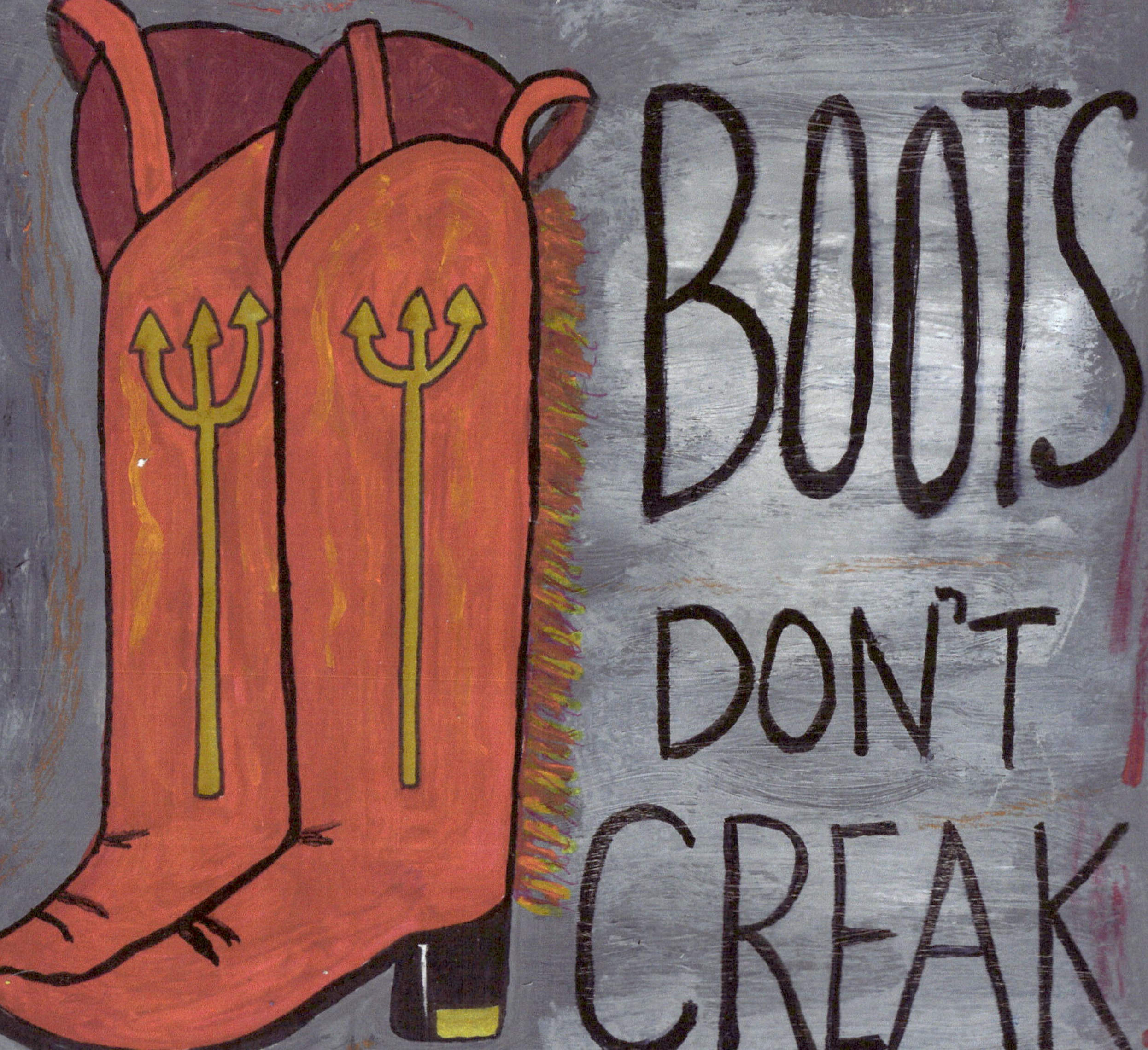

THE DEVIL'S
BOOTS
DON'T
CREAK
~Scottish Proverb
20

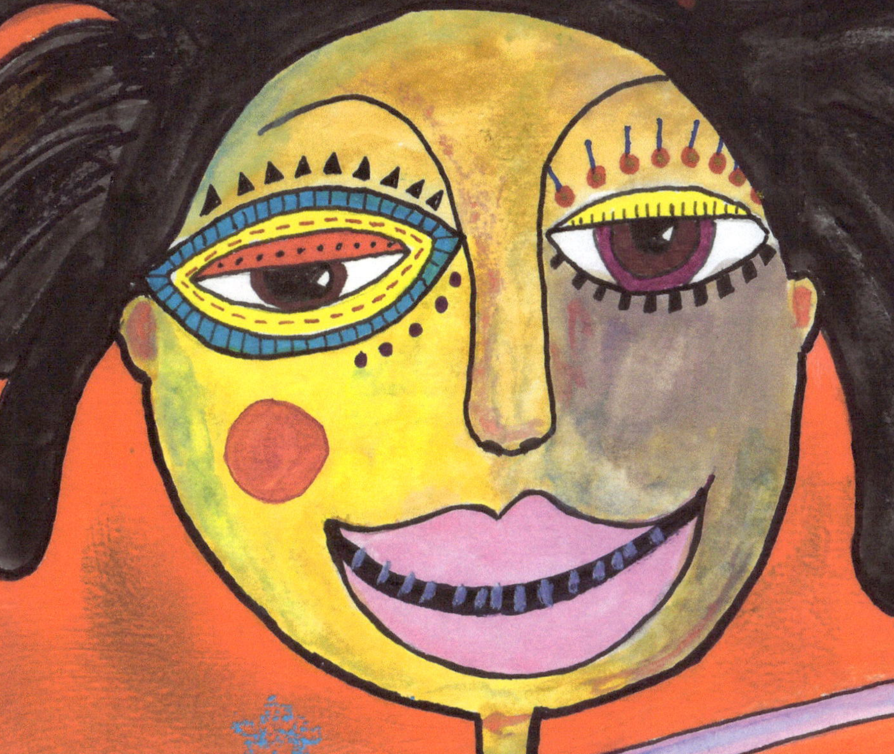

WORK...
UNTIL
YOU
NO LONGER
HAVE TO
INTRODUCE YOURSELF.

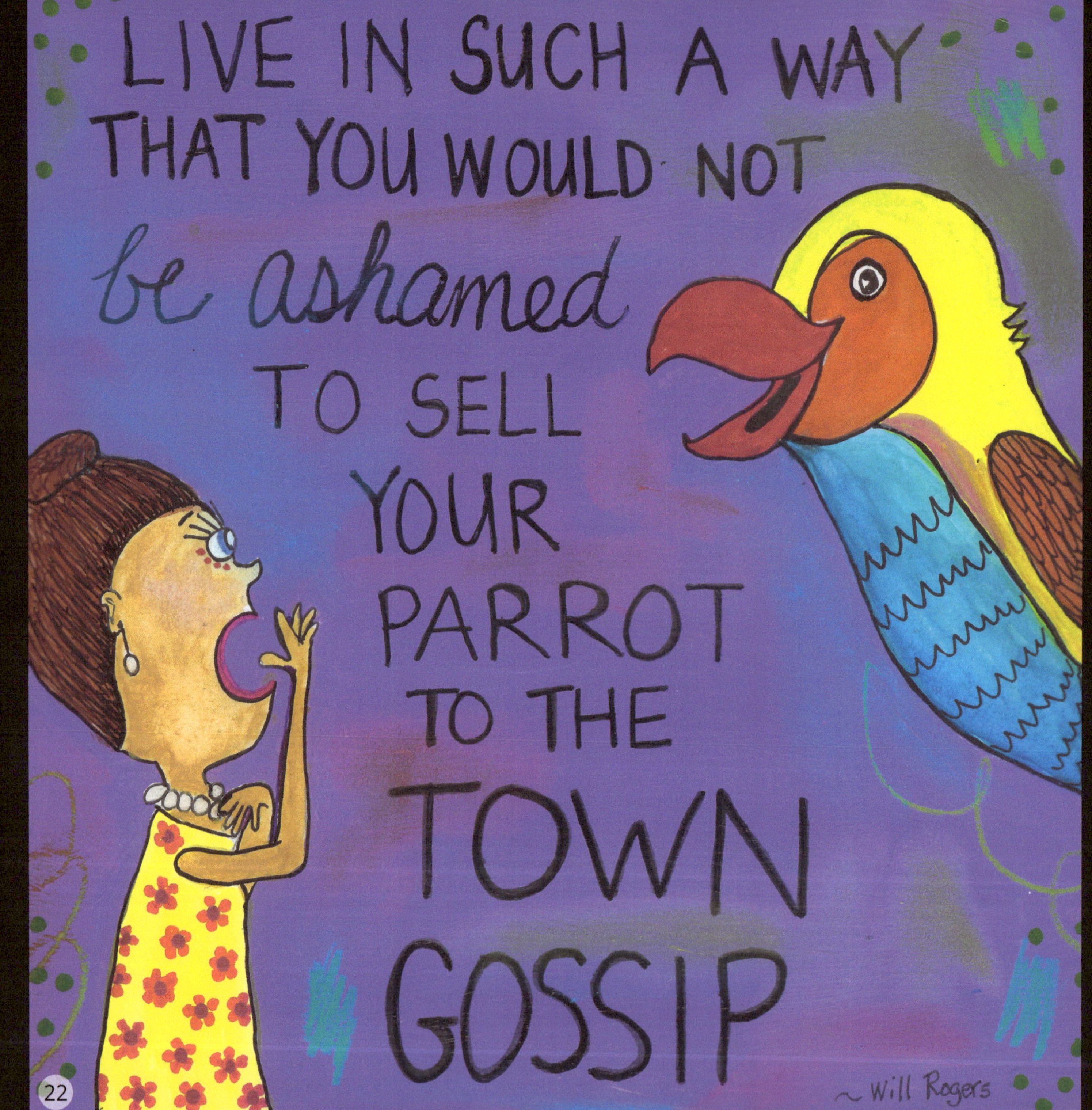

LIVE IN SUCH A WAY
THAT YOU WOULD NOT
be ashamed
TO SELL
YOUR
PARROT
TO THE
TOWN
GOSSIP
~ Will Rogers
22

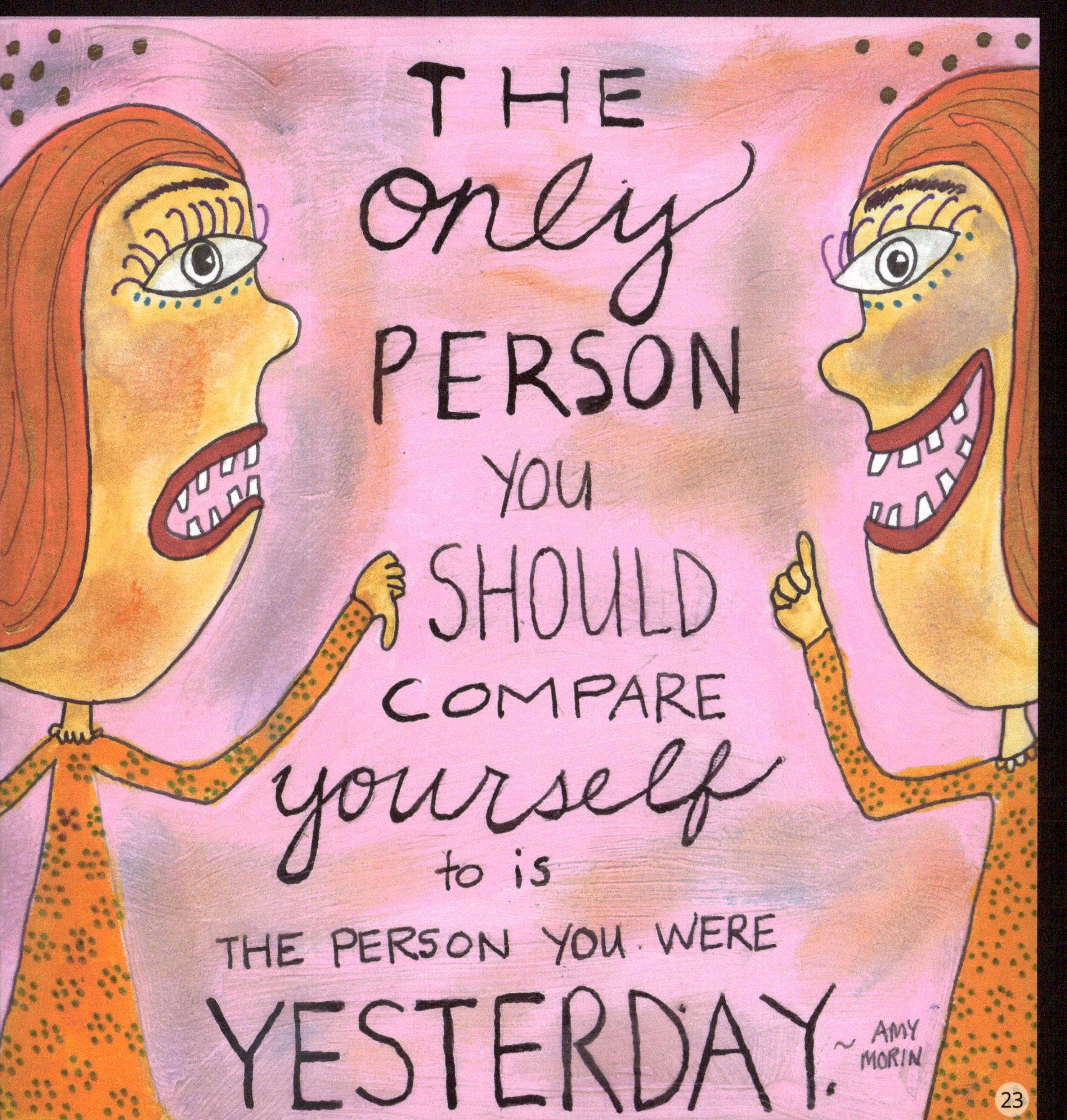

THE only PERSON YOU SHOULD COMPARE yourself to is THE PERSON YOU WERE YESTERDAY.
~ AMY MORIN
23

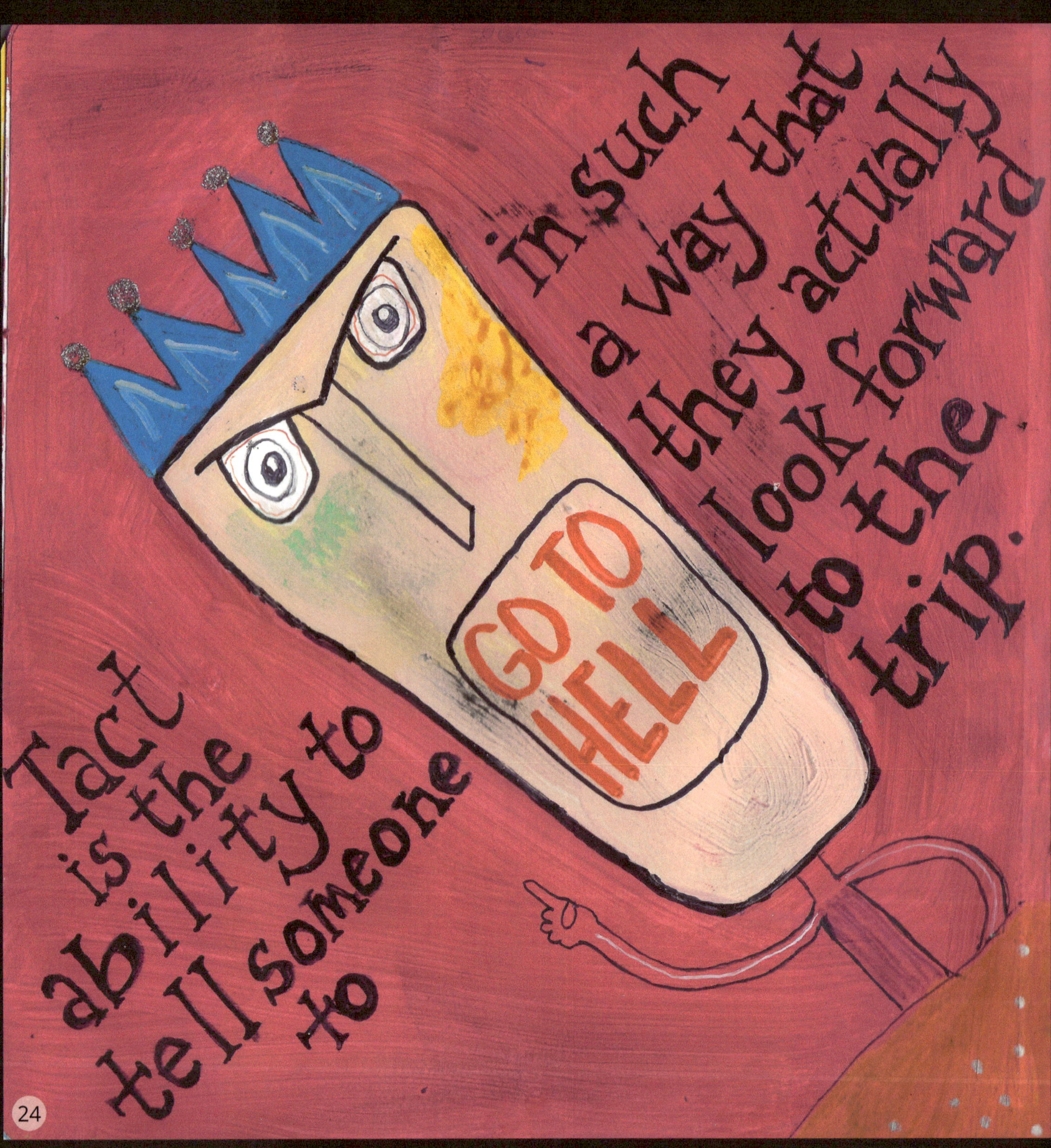

Tact is the ability to tell someone to
GO TO HELL
in such a way that they actually look forward to the trip.
24

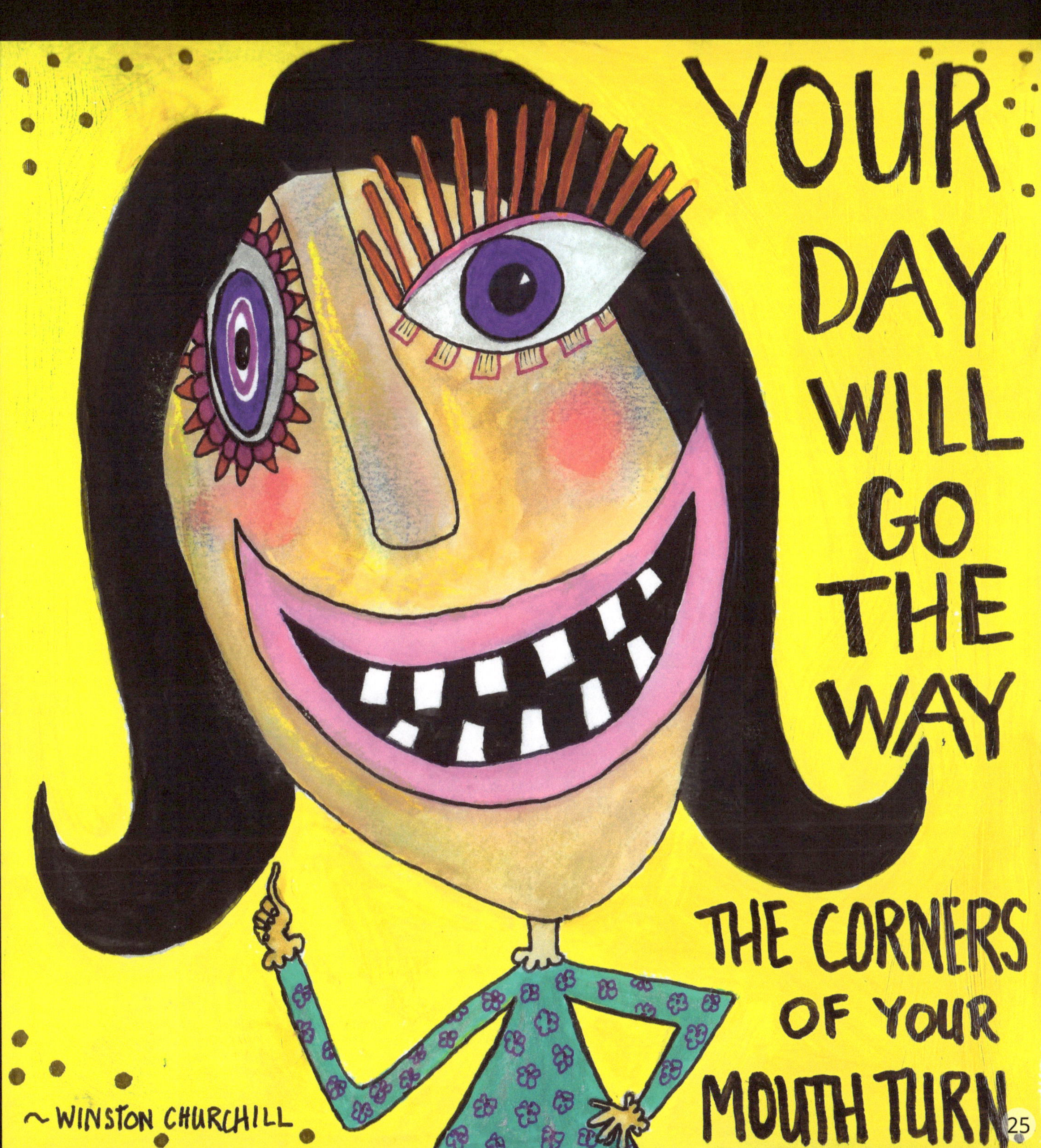
YOUR
DAY
WILL
GO
THE
WAY
THE CORNERS
OF YOUR
MOUTH TURN
~ WINSTON CHURCHILL
25

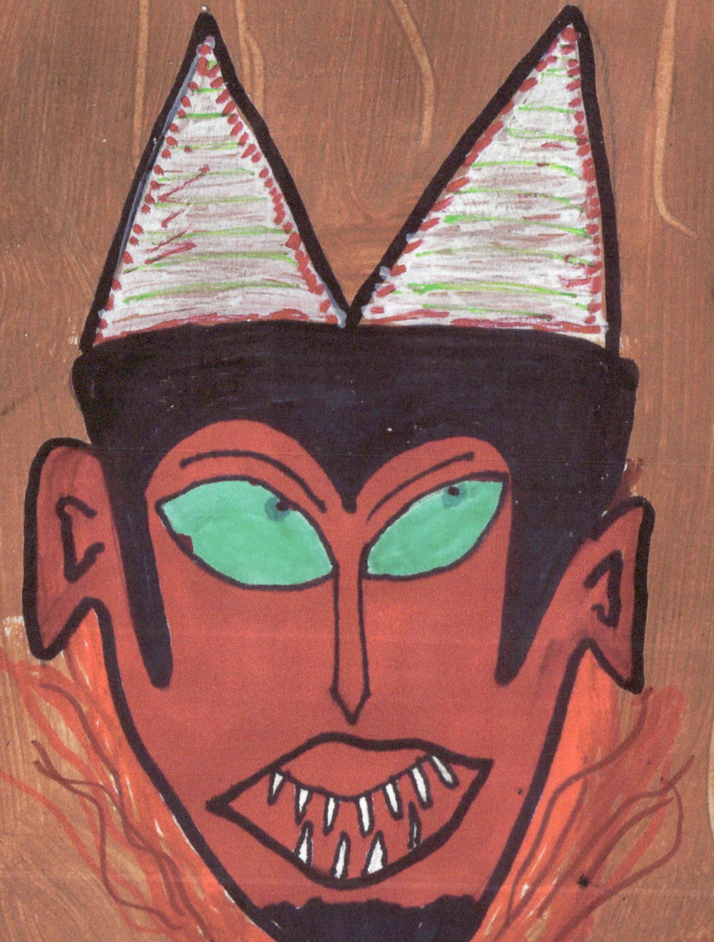

Resist the devil, and he will flee from you.
James 4:7
26

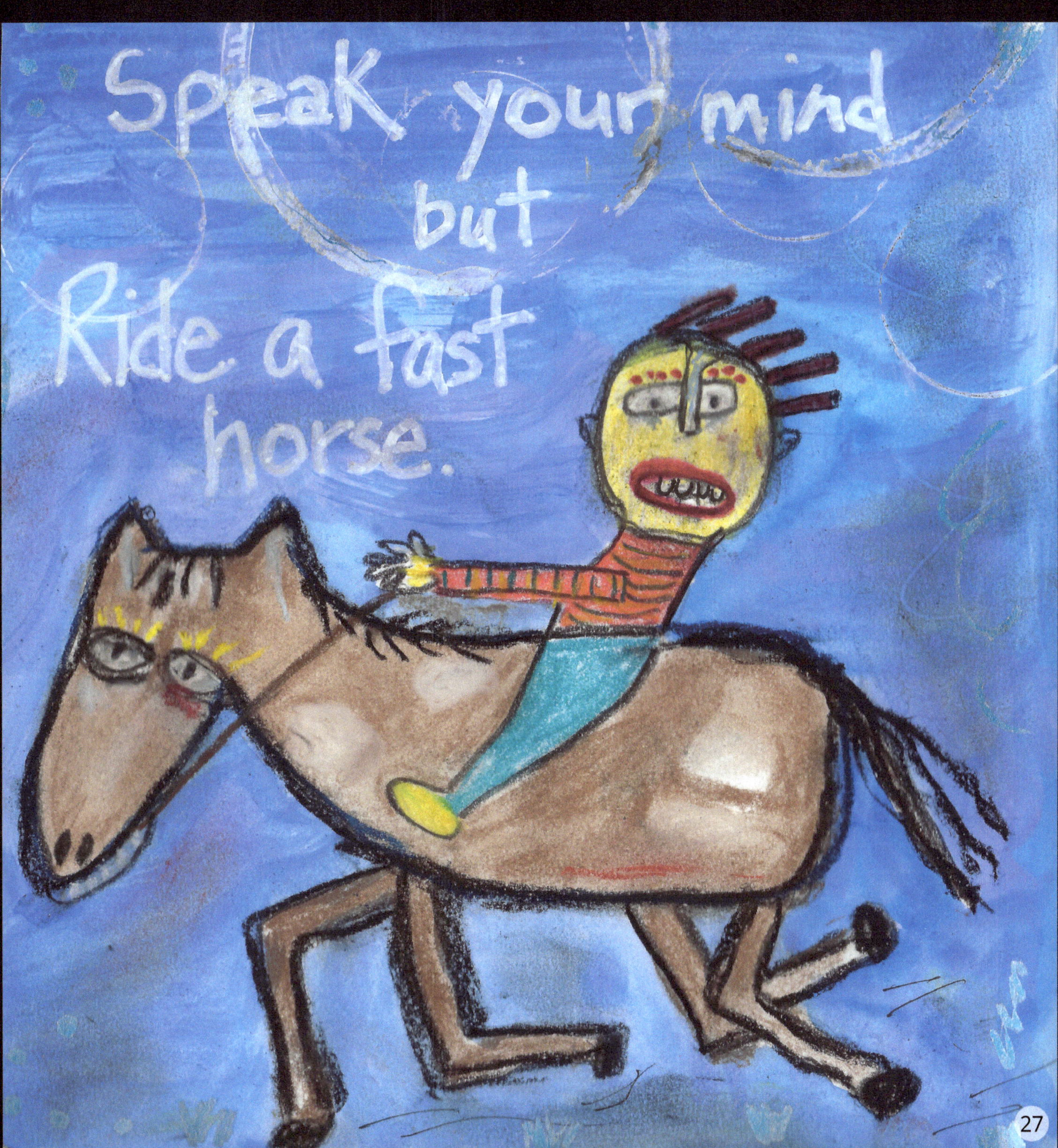

Speak your mind
but
Ride a fast
horse.
27

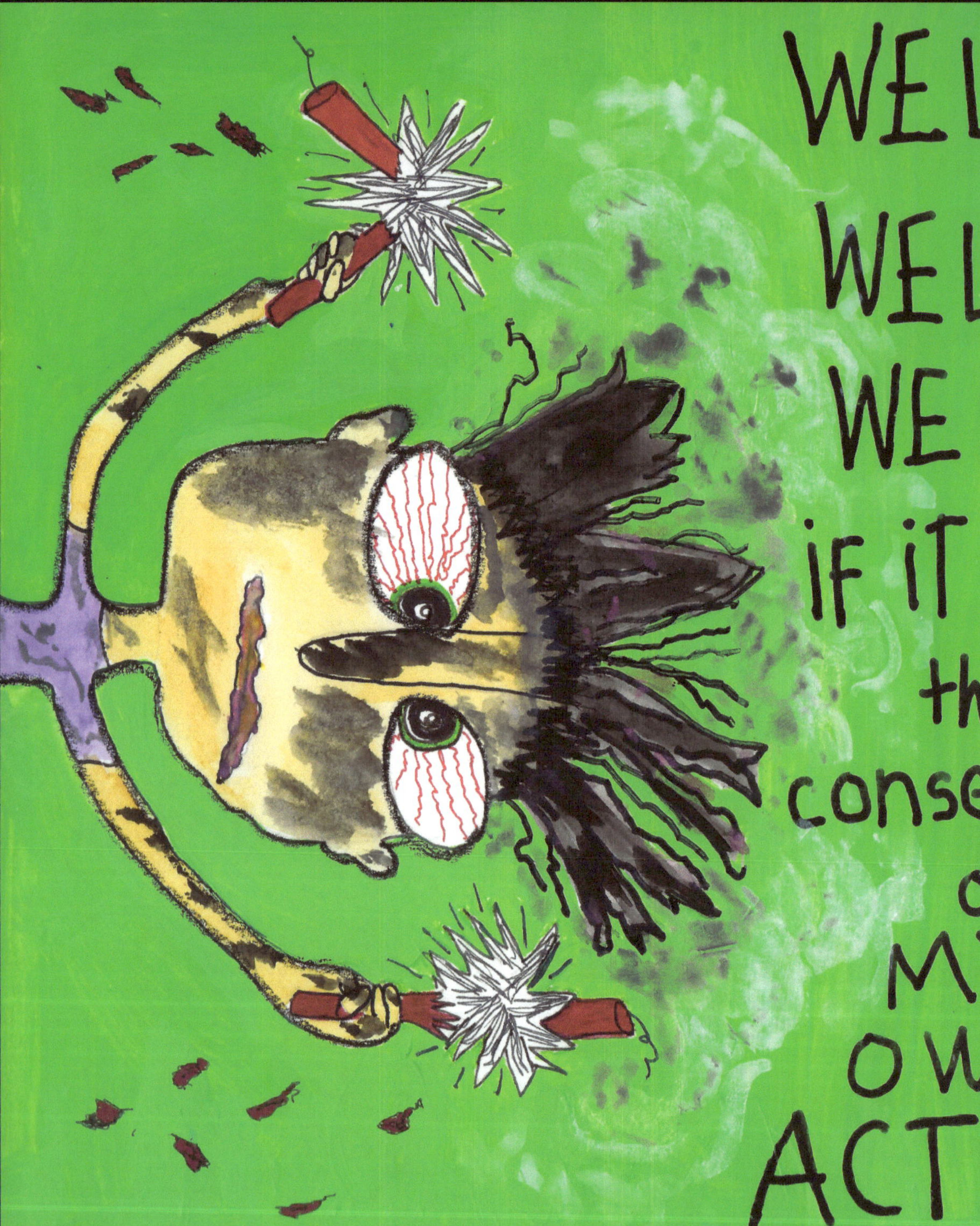

WELL,
WELL,
WELL.
if it isn't
the
consequences
of
MY
OWN
ACTIONS.

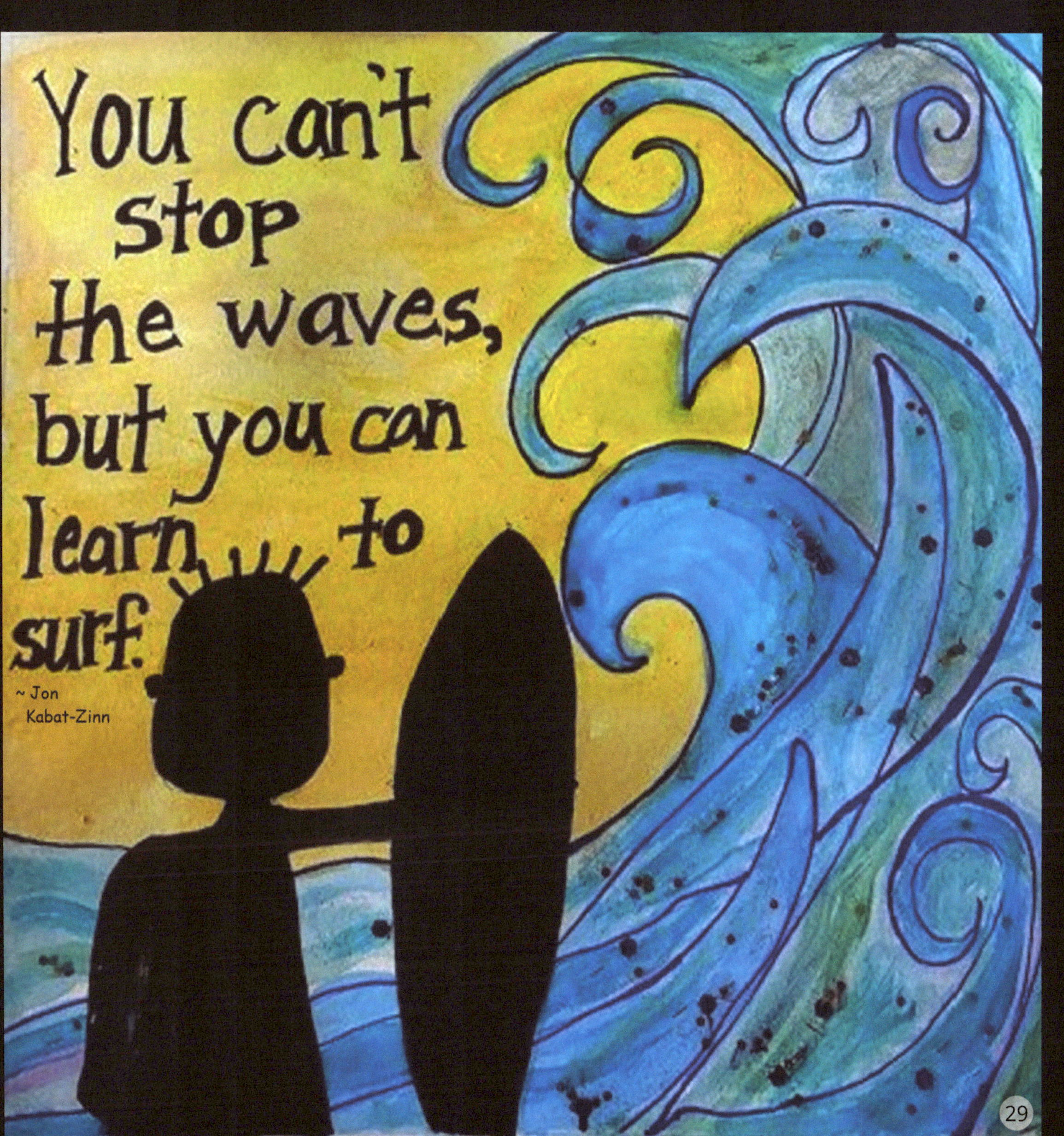

You can't stop the waves, but you can learn to surf.
~ Jon Kabat-Zinn

EVERYONE
has a plan
UNTIL
THEY
GET
PUNCHED
in the
FACE
30

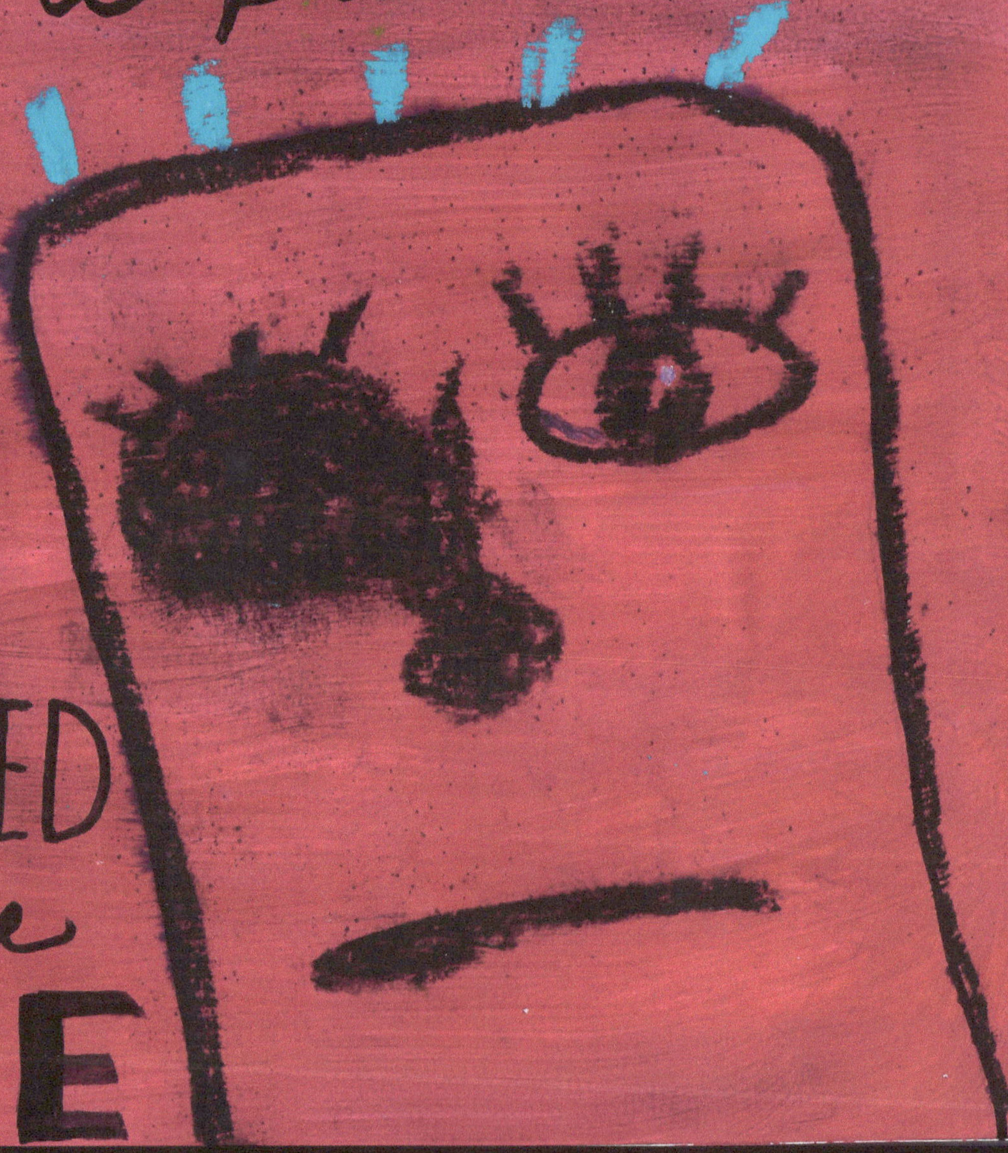

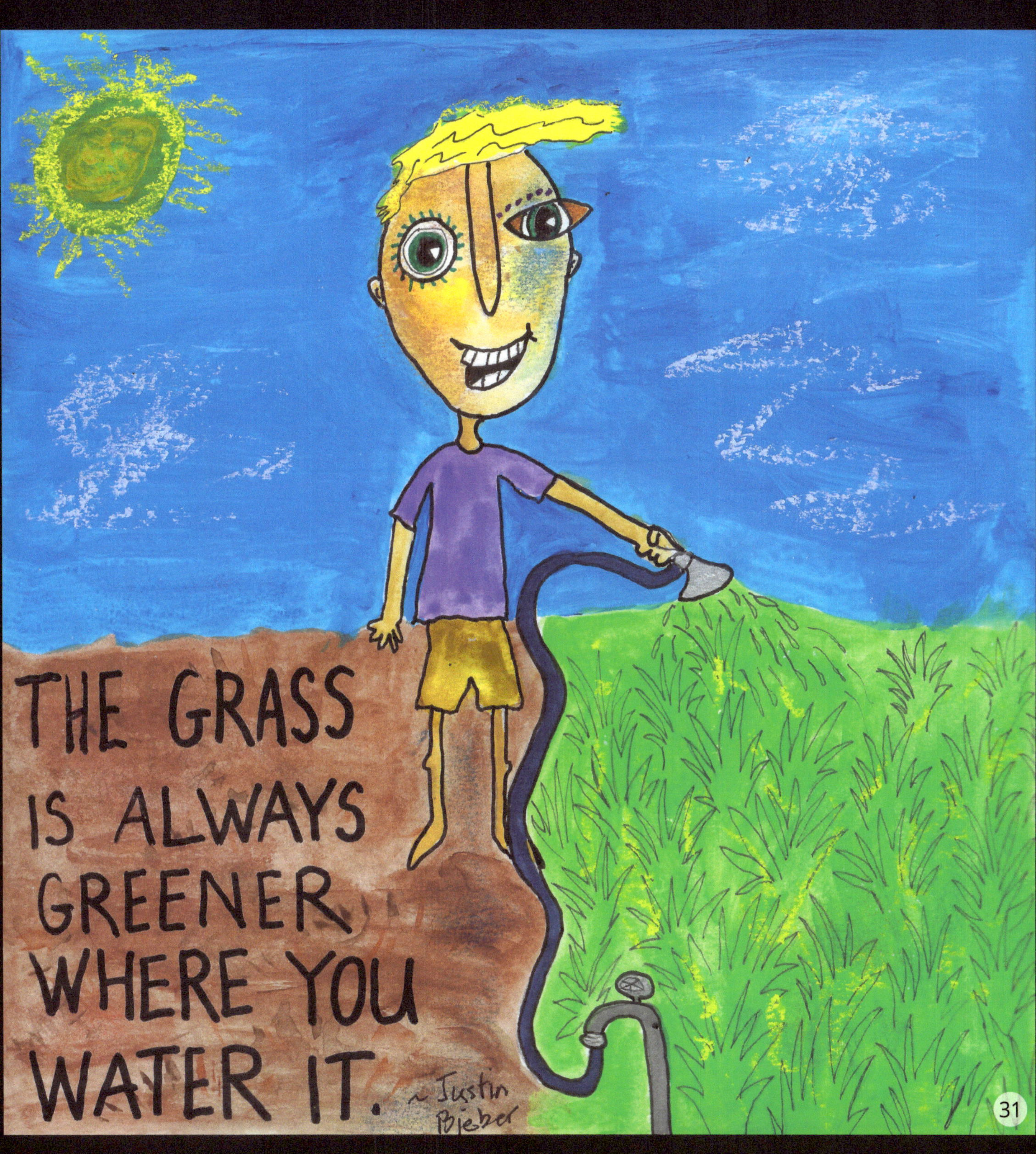

THE GRASS
IS ALWAYS
GREENER
WHERE YOU
WATER IT.
~ Justin
Bieber
31

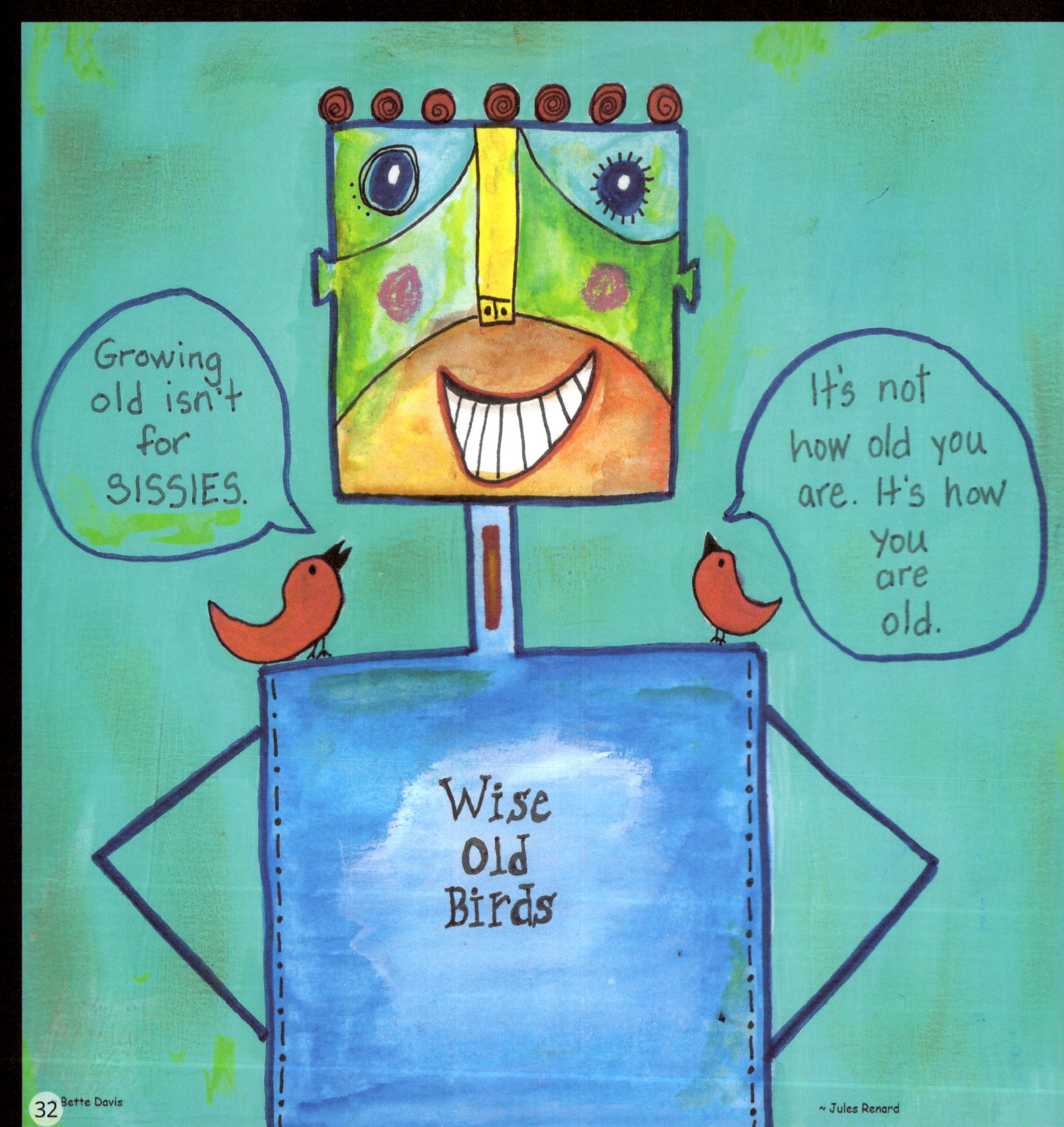

Growing
old isn't
for
SISSIES.

It's not
how old you
are. It's how
you
are
old.

Wise
Old
Birds

Bette Davis

~ Jules Renard

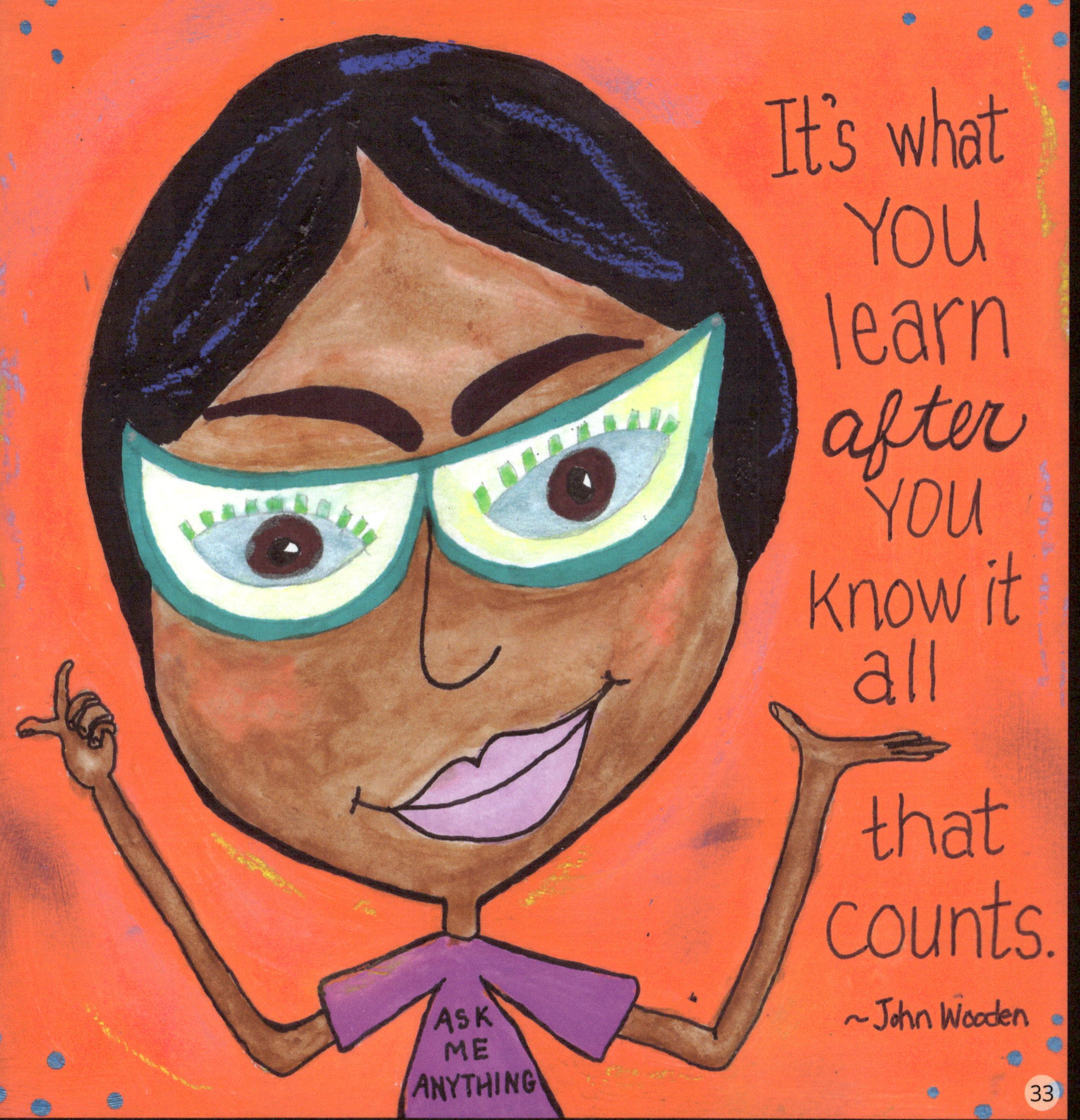
It's what
you
learn
after
you
know it
all
that
counts.
~John Wooden
ASK ME ANYTHING
33

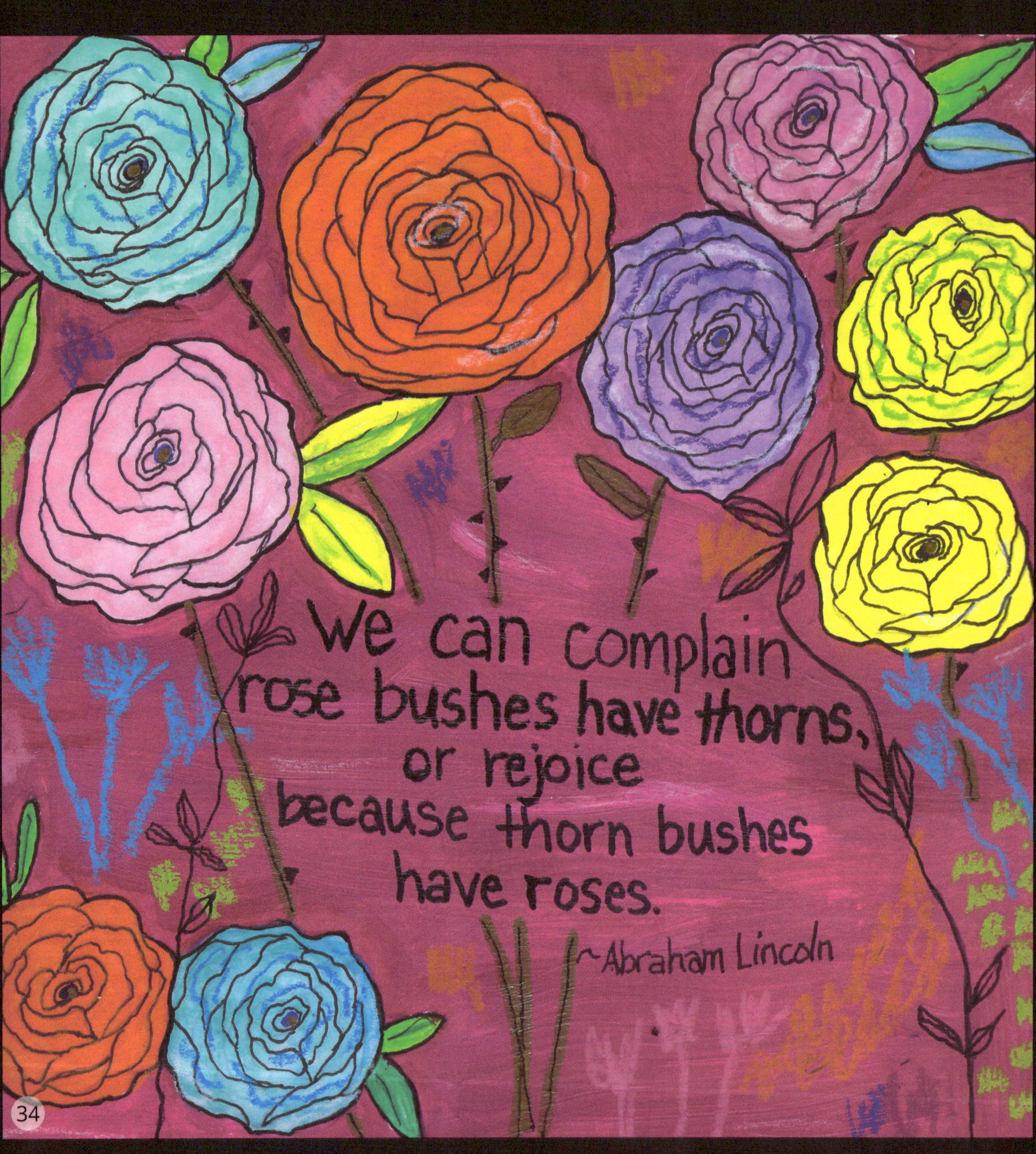

We can complain
rose bushes have thorns,
or rejoice
because thorn bushes
have roses.
~Abraham Lincoln

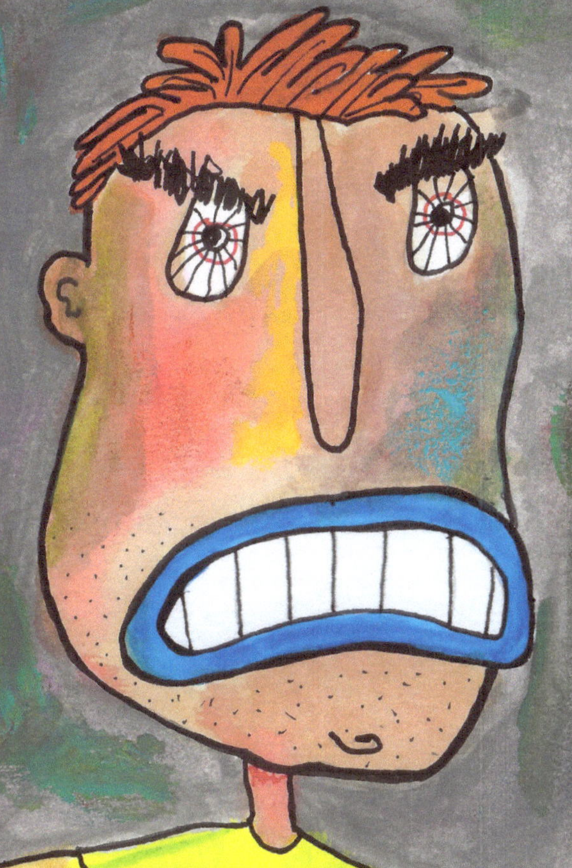
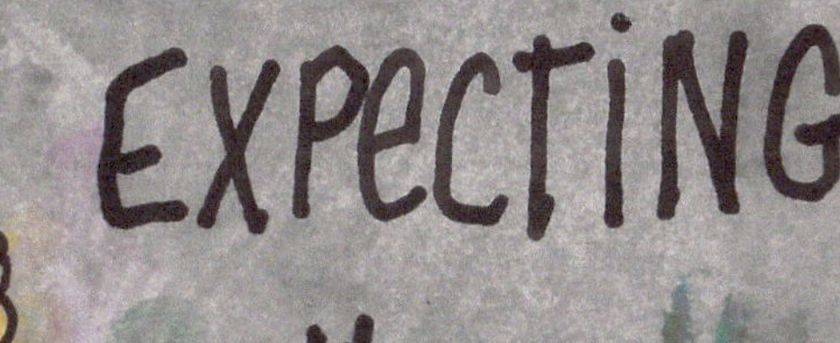
HOLDING ONTO ANGER
is LIKE
DRINKING
Poison
and
EXPECTING
the
OTHER
PERSON
TO DIE.
POISON
~ Malachy McCourt

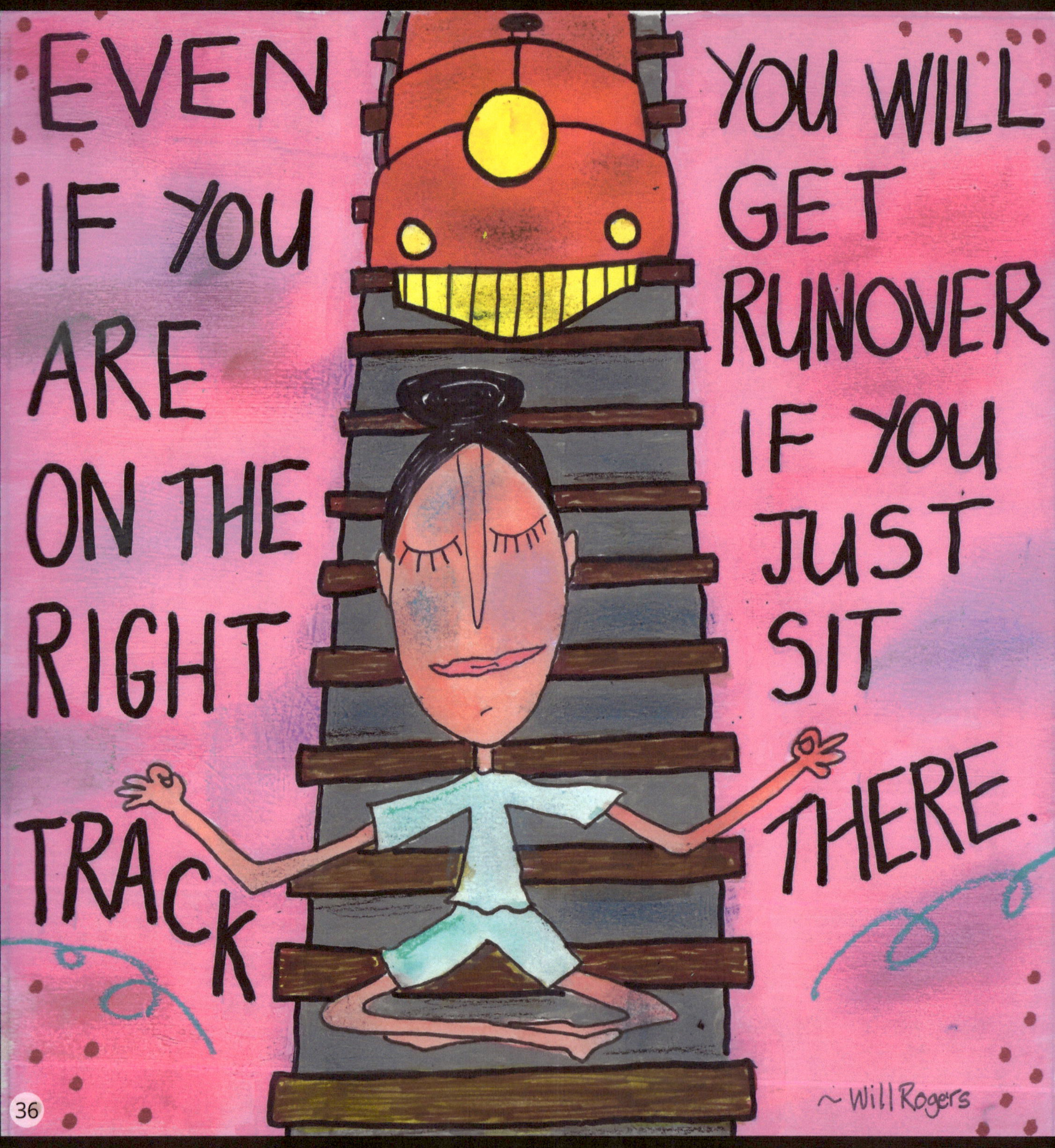

EVEN IF YOU ARE ON THE RIGHT TRACK
YOU WILL GET RUNOVER IF YOU JUST SIT THERE.
~ Will Rogers
36

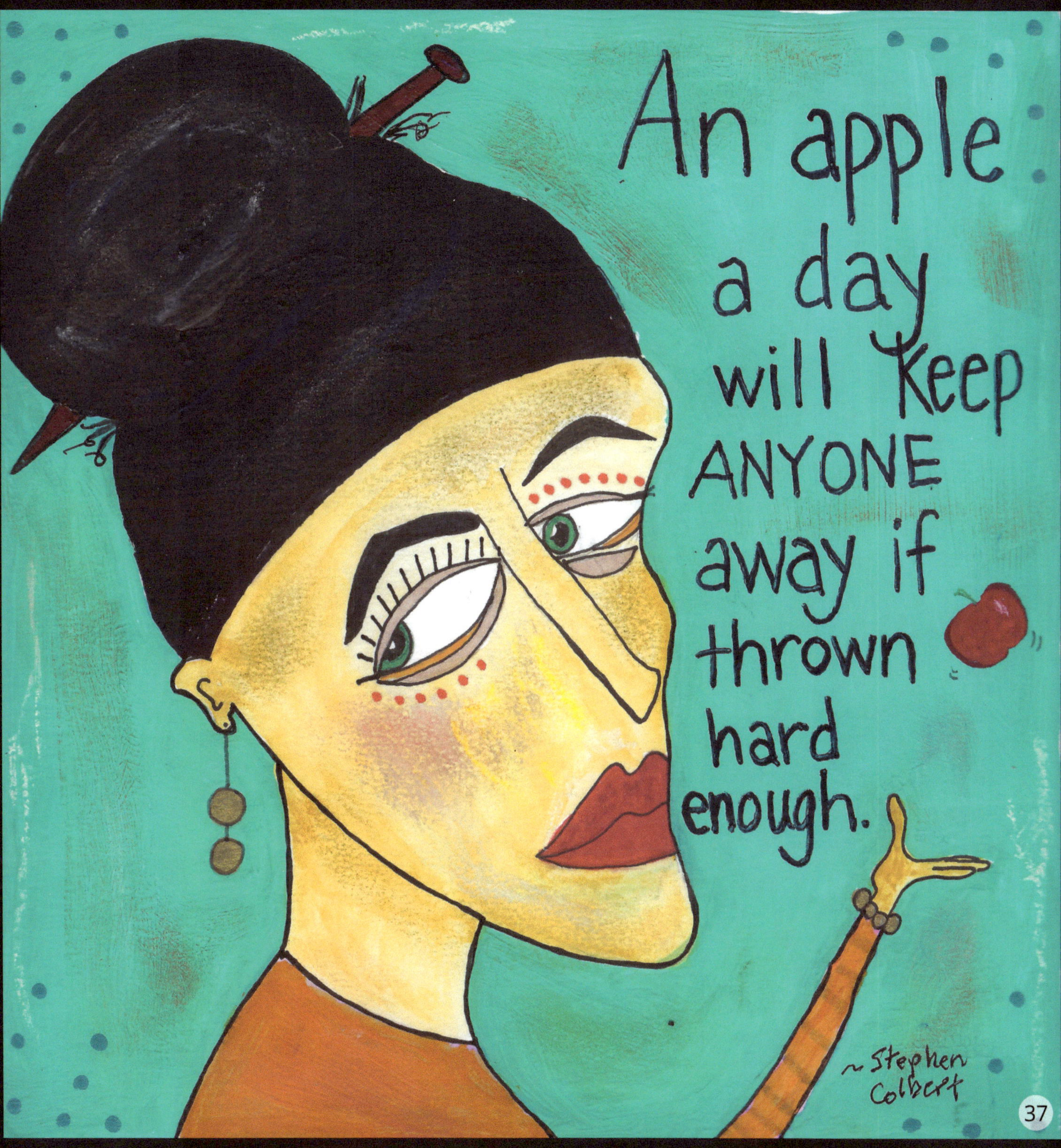

An apple a day will keep ANYONE away if thrown hard enough.
~ Stephen Colbert
37

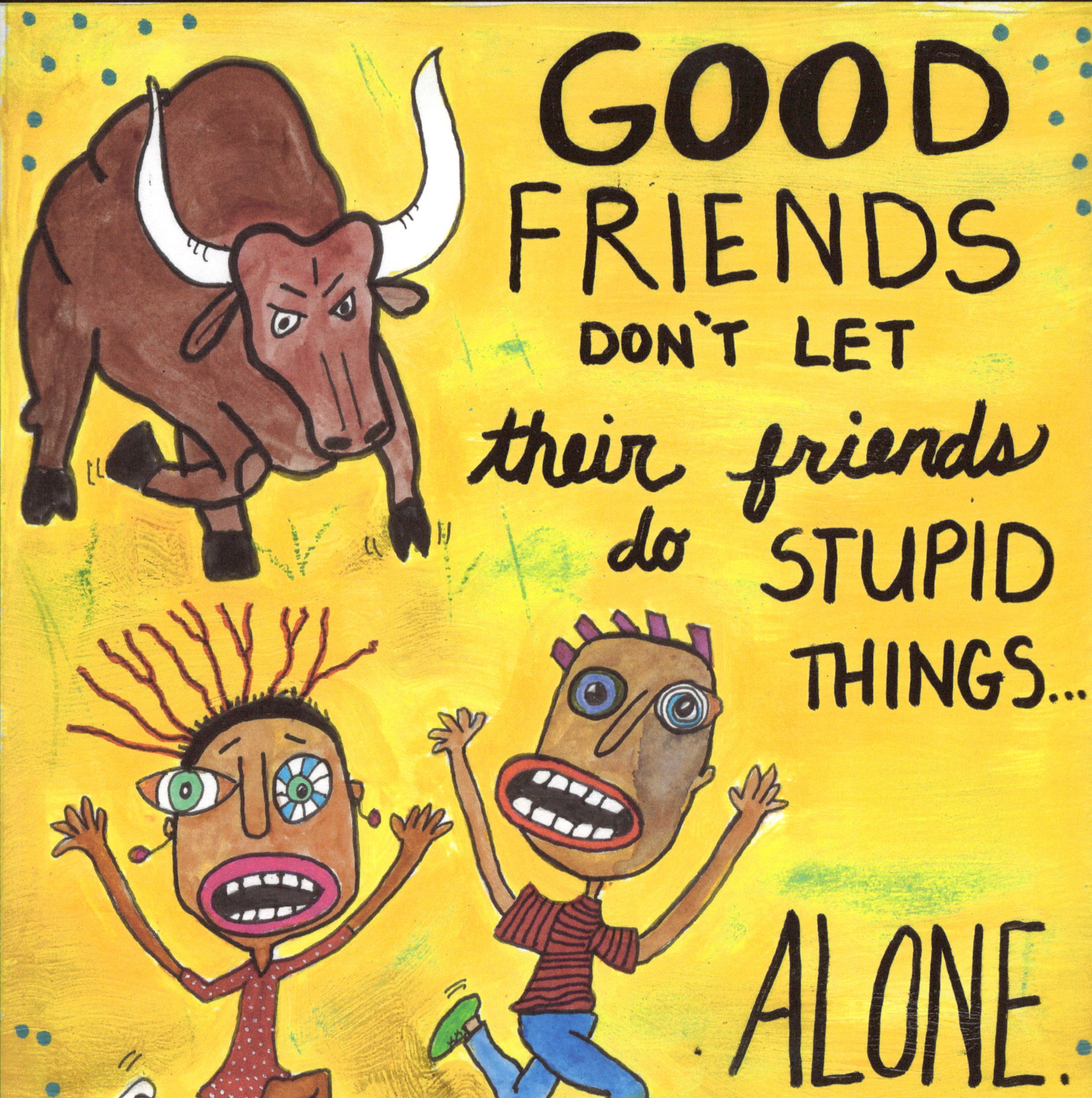

GOOD
FRIENDS
DON'T LET
their friends
do STUPID
THINGS...
ALONE.
~Ain Eineziz
38

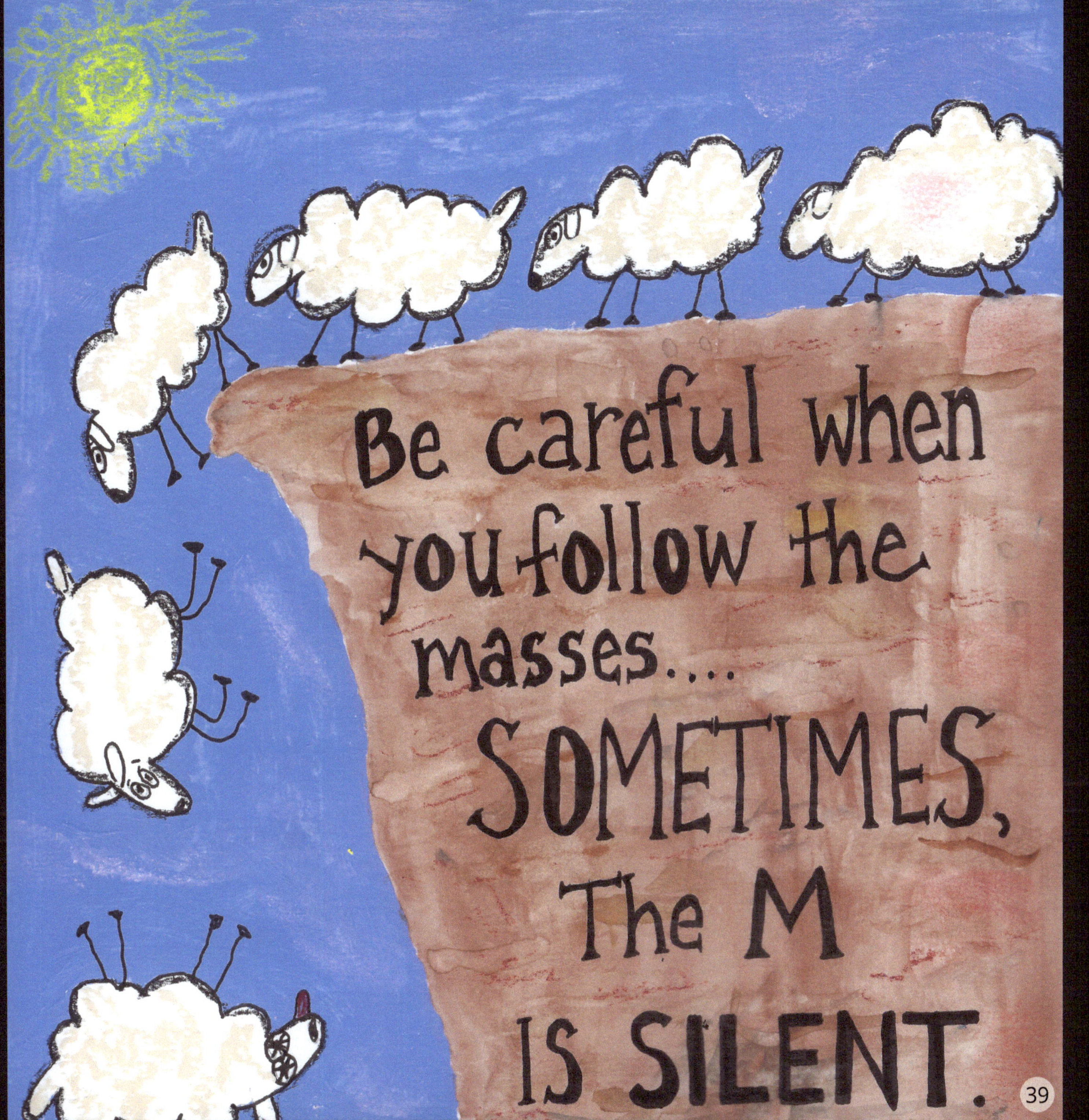
Be careful when you follow the masses....
SOMETIMES, The M IS SILENT.

If
IFs and BUTs
were
candy & nuts,
we'd have
A PARTY
wouldn't
we?
IF
BUT
BUT
IF
BUT
IF
BUT
BUT
IF
BUT
BUT
BUT

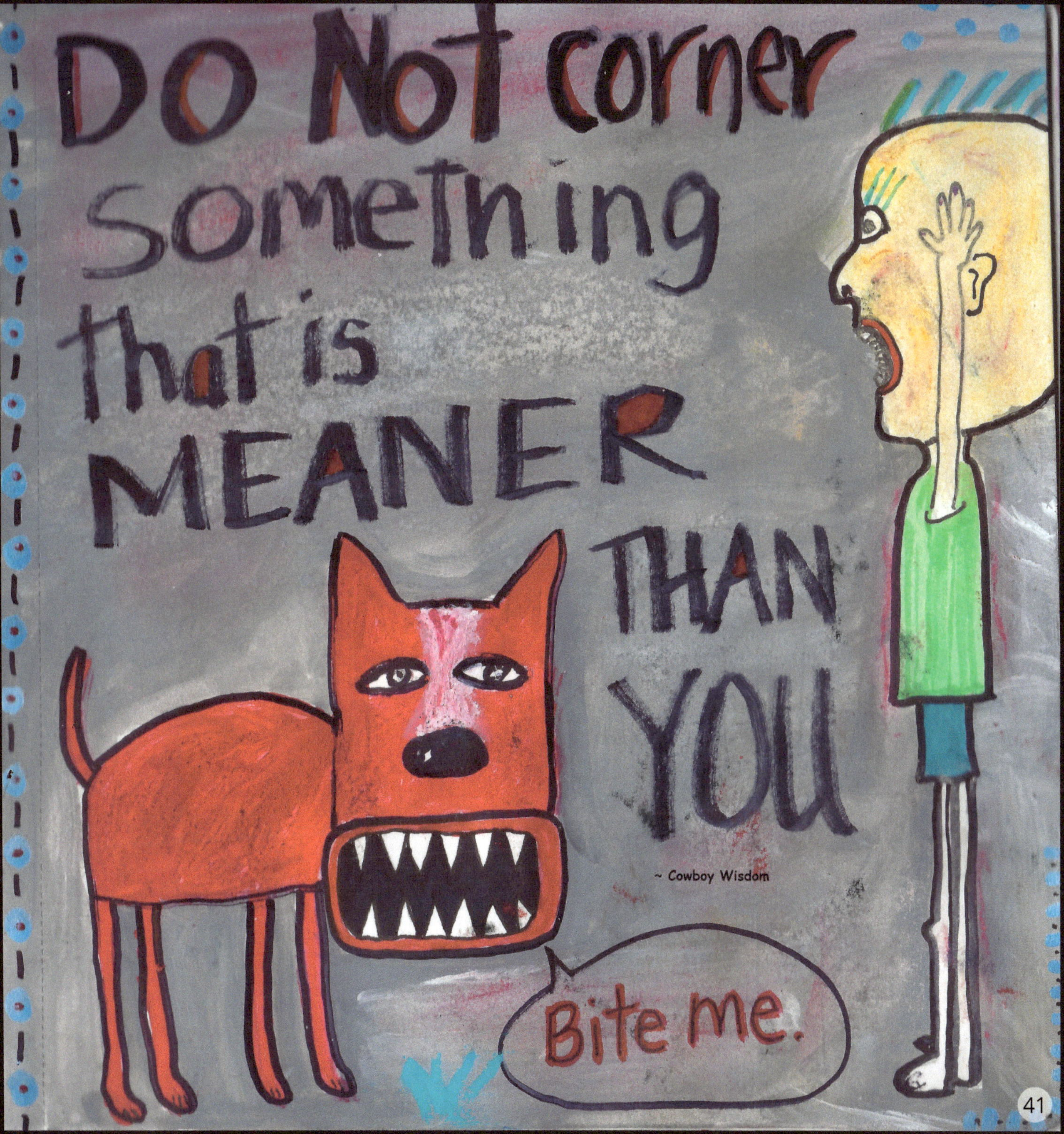

Do Not corner
Something
that is
MEANER
THAN
YOU
~ Cowboy Wisdom
Bite me.

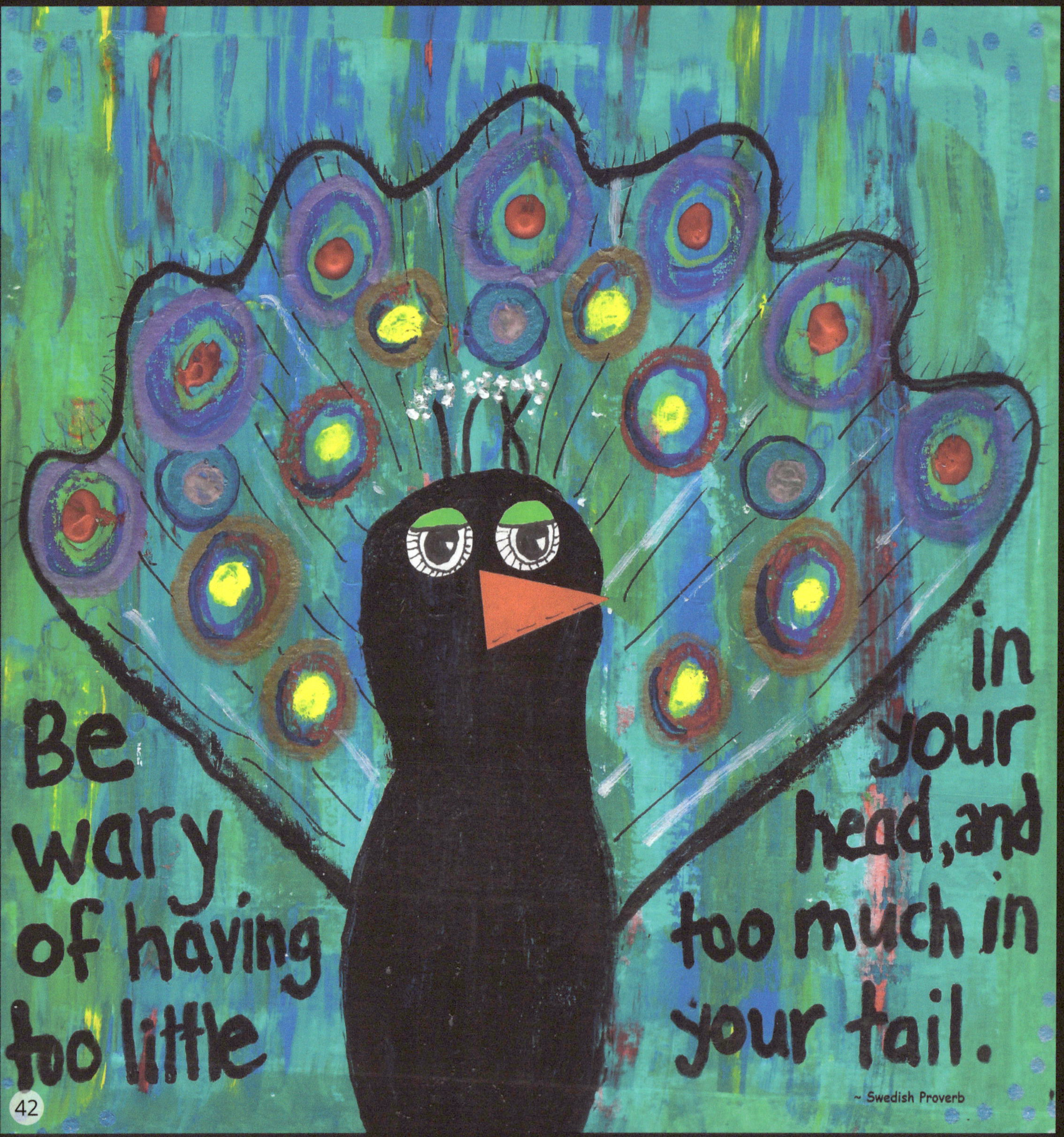

Be wary of having too little
in your head, and too much in your tail.
~ Swedish Proverb

Don't Raise your voice...

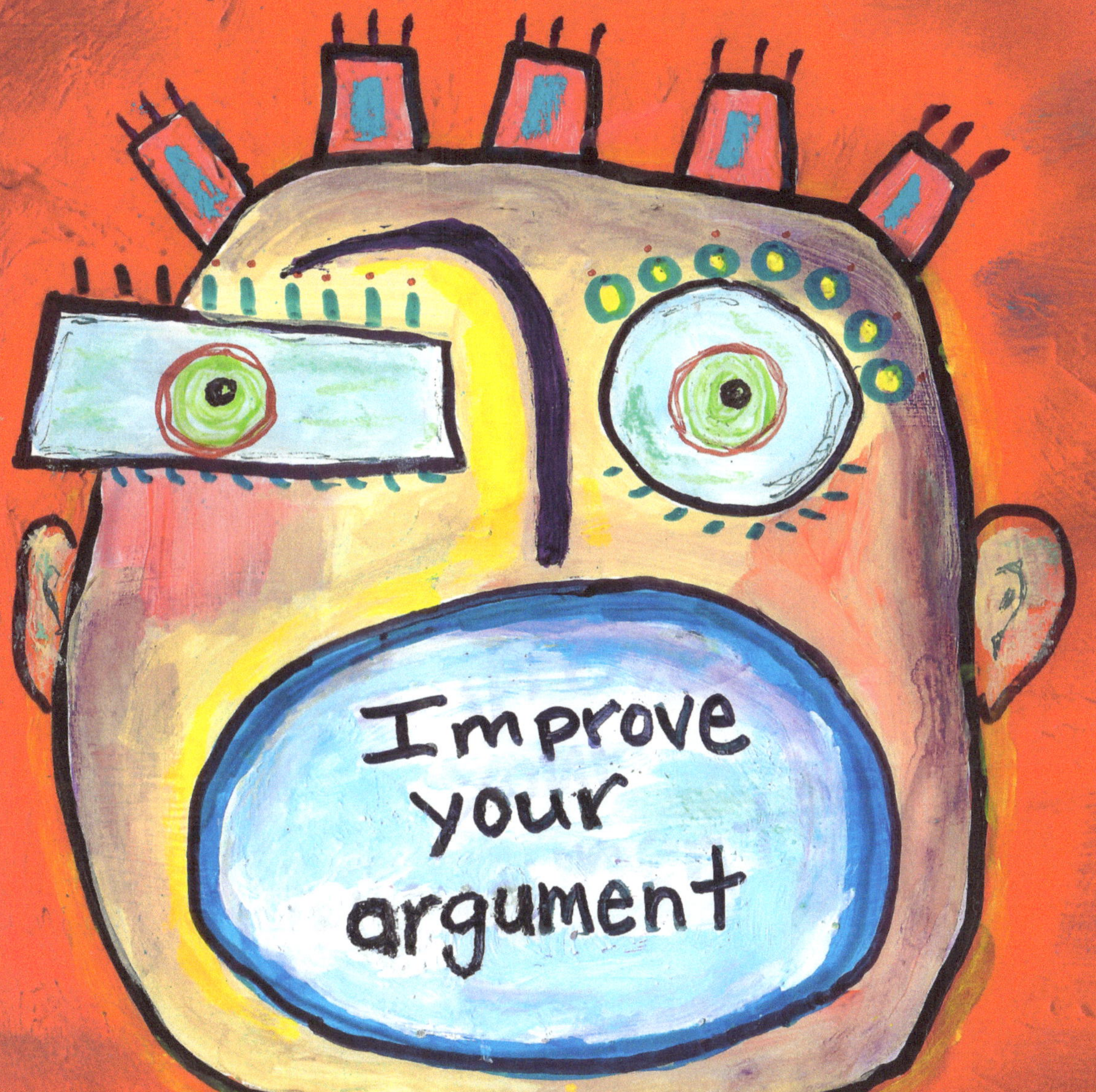

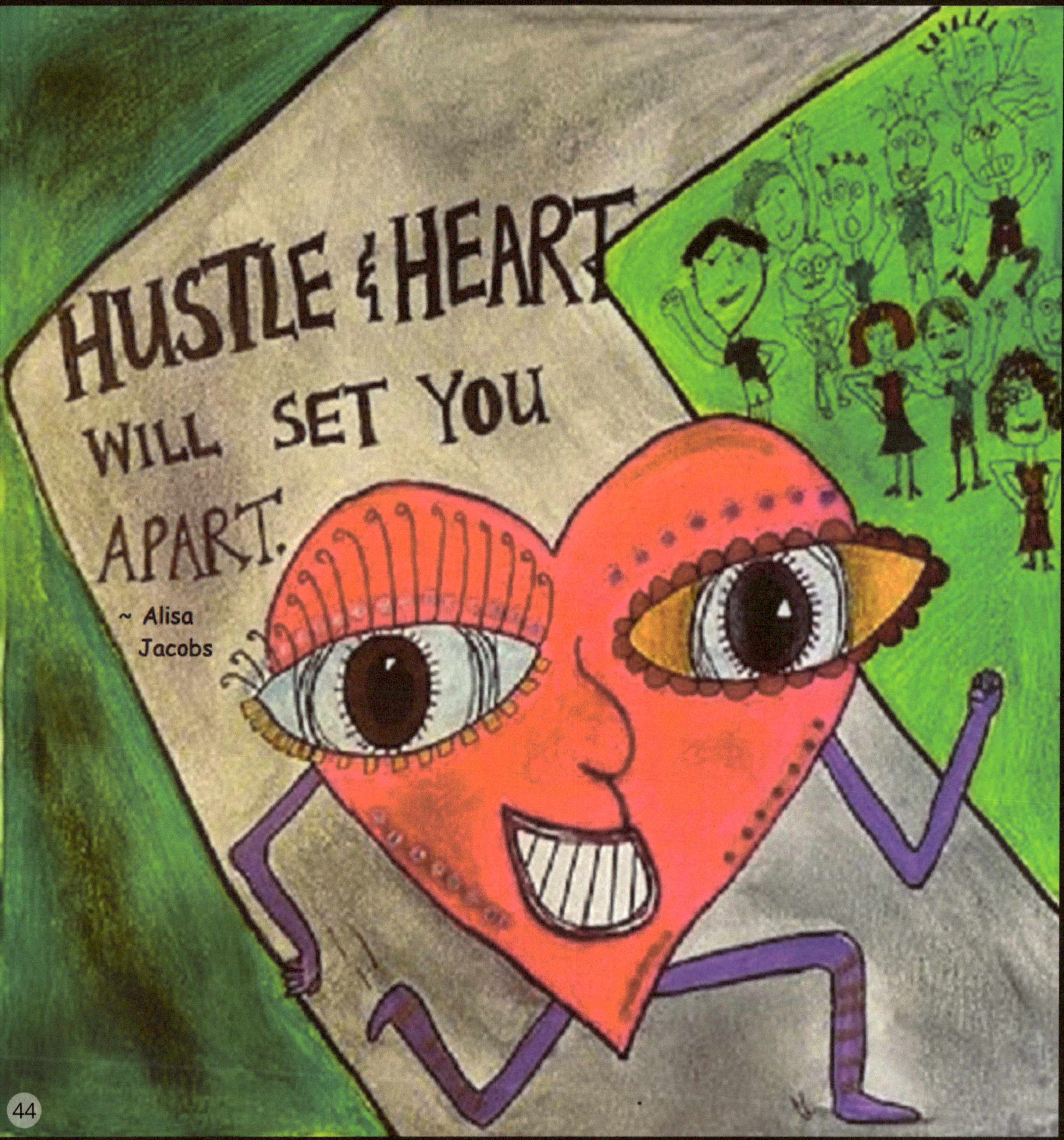

HUSTLE & HEART
WILL SET YOU
APART.
~ Alisa
Jacobs

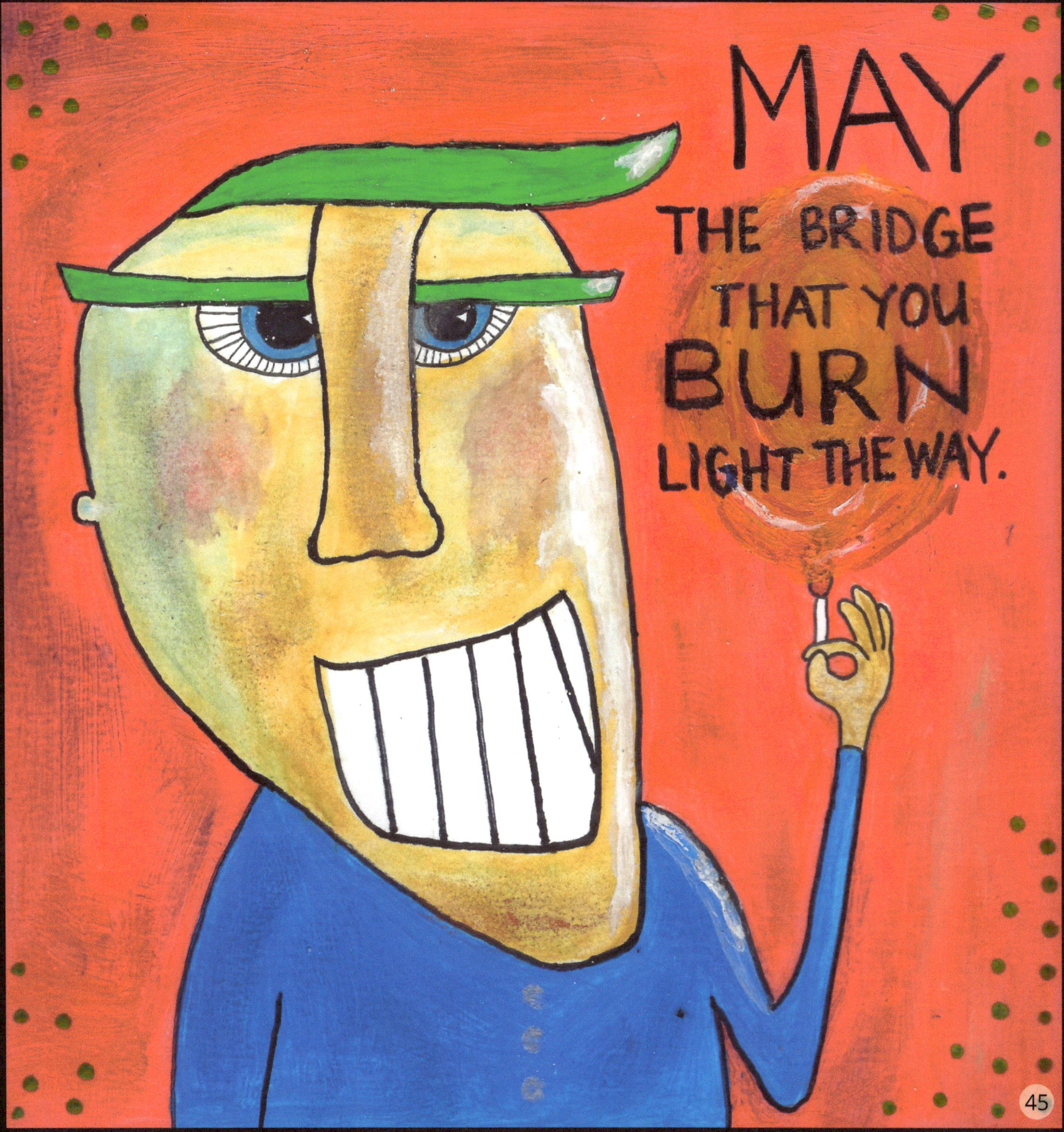

MAY
THE BRIDGE
THAT YOU
BURN
LIGHT THE WAY.

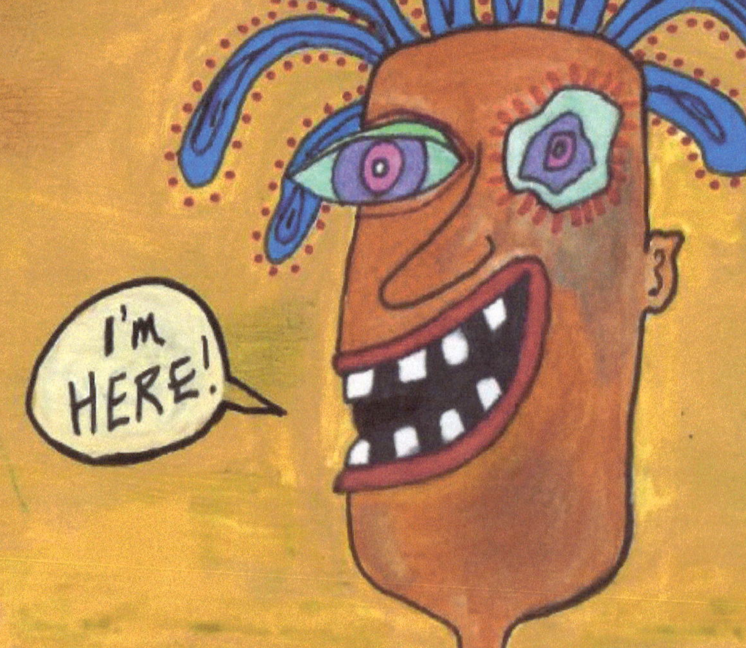

80% of Success is
I'M HERE!
SHOWING UP.
~Woody Allen

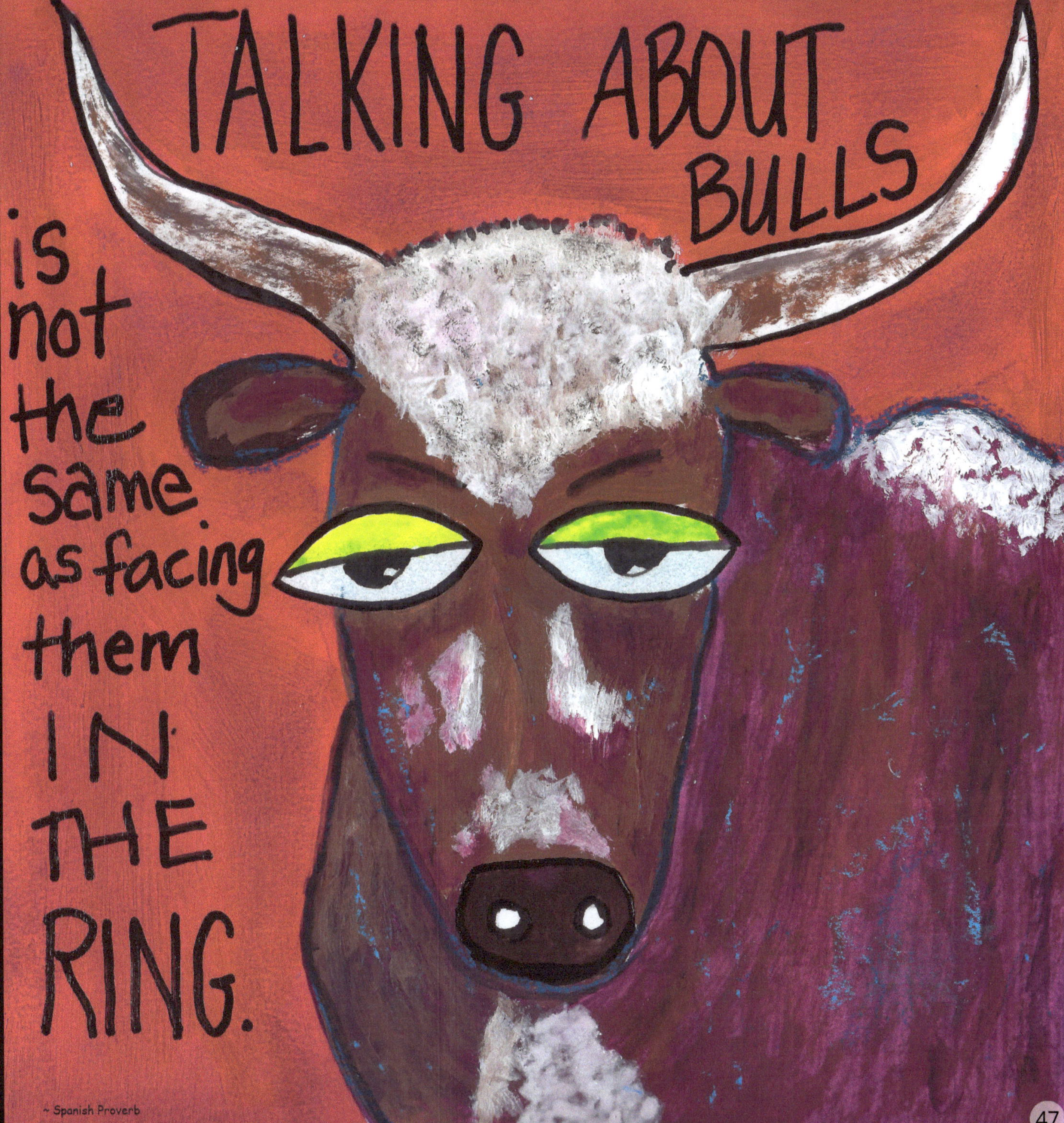

TALKING ABOUT BULLS
is not the same as facing them IN THE RING.
~ Spanish Proverb
47

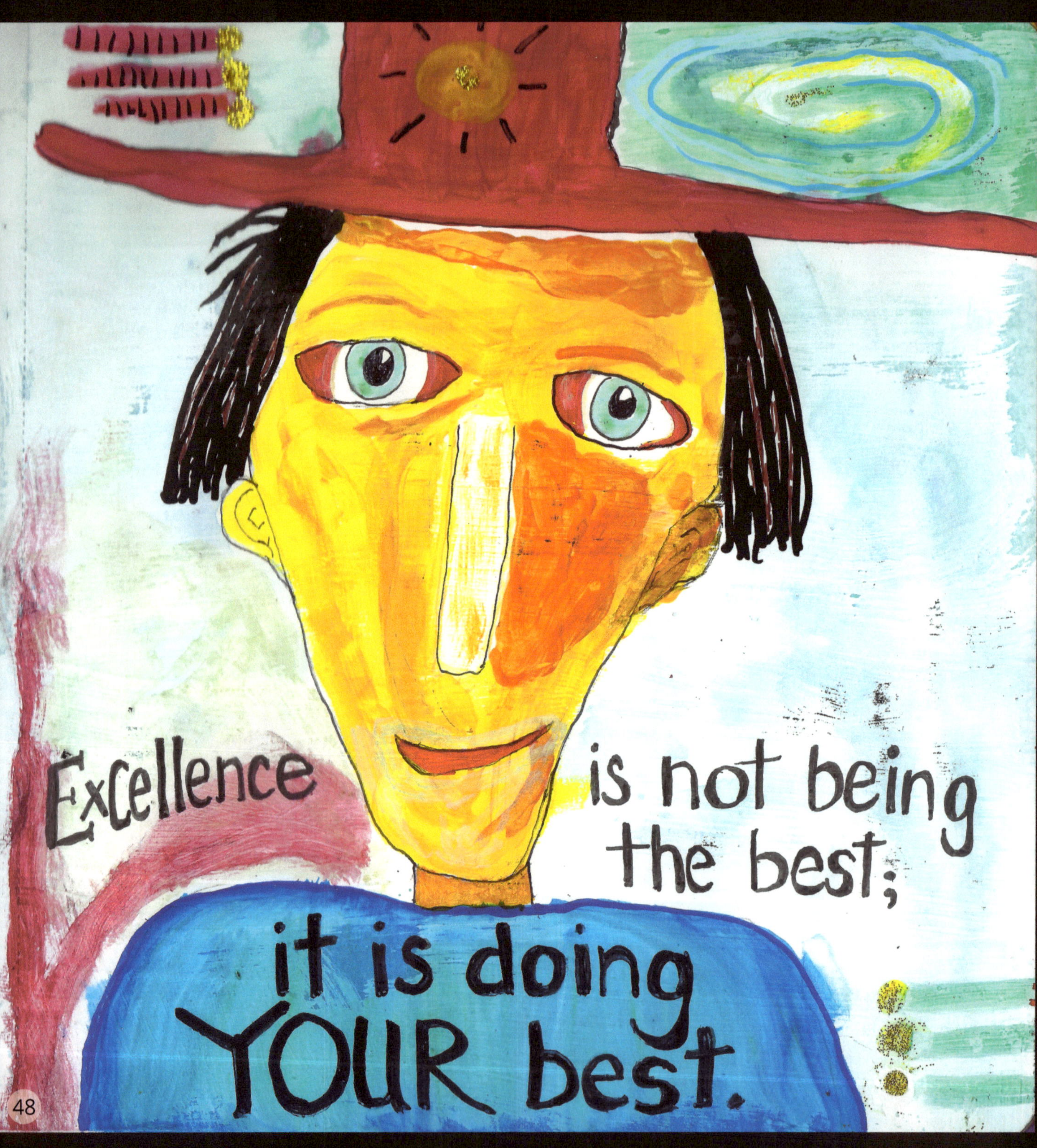

Excellence is not being the best; it is doing YOUR best.

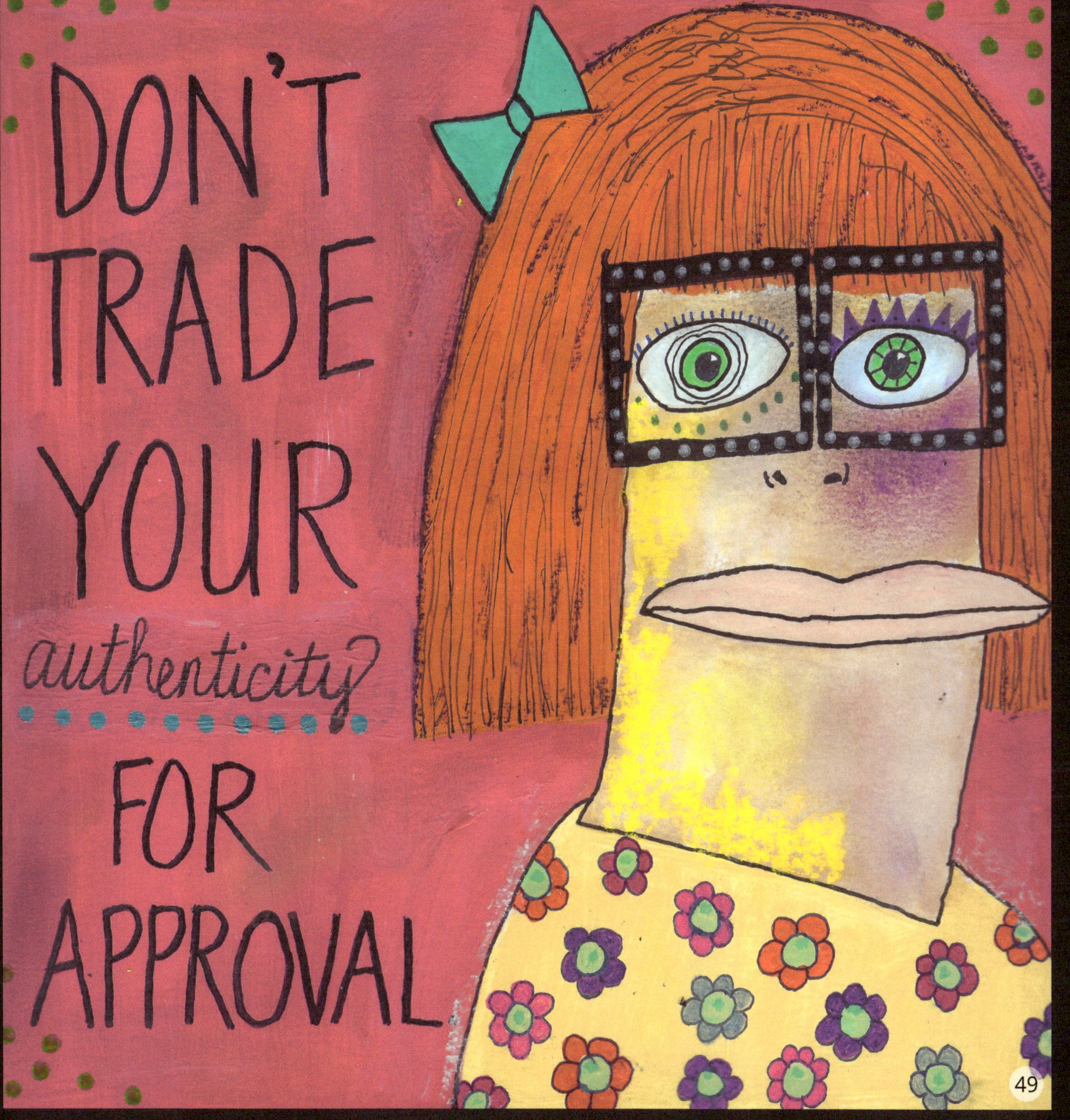

DON'T
TRADE
YOUR
authenticity
FOR
APPROVAL

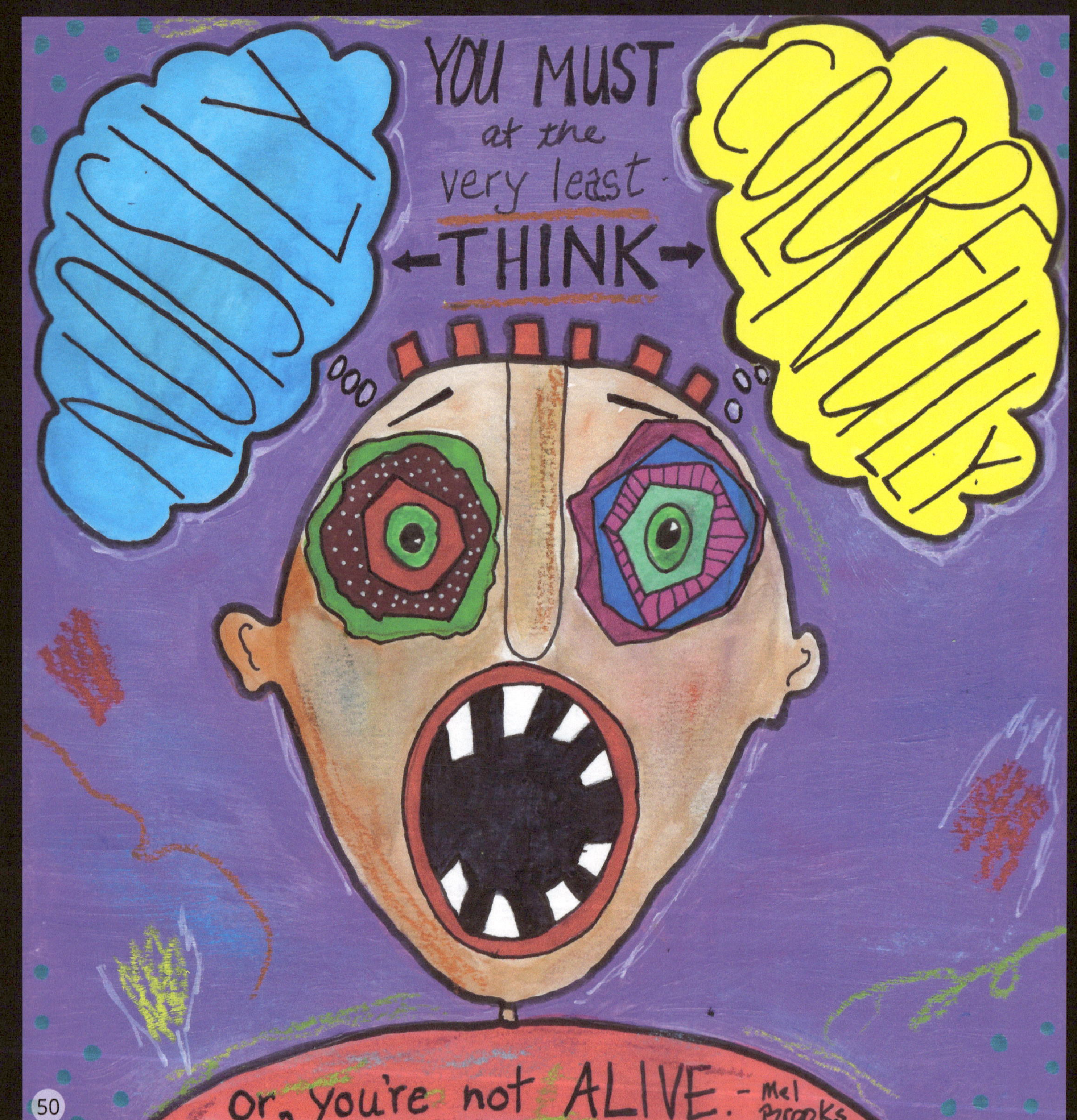

NOISILY
YOU MUST
at the
very least.
←THINK→
QUIETLY
Or, you're not ALIVE. —Mel Brooks
50

MAKE SURE YOUR

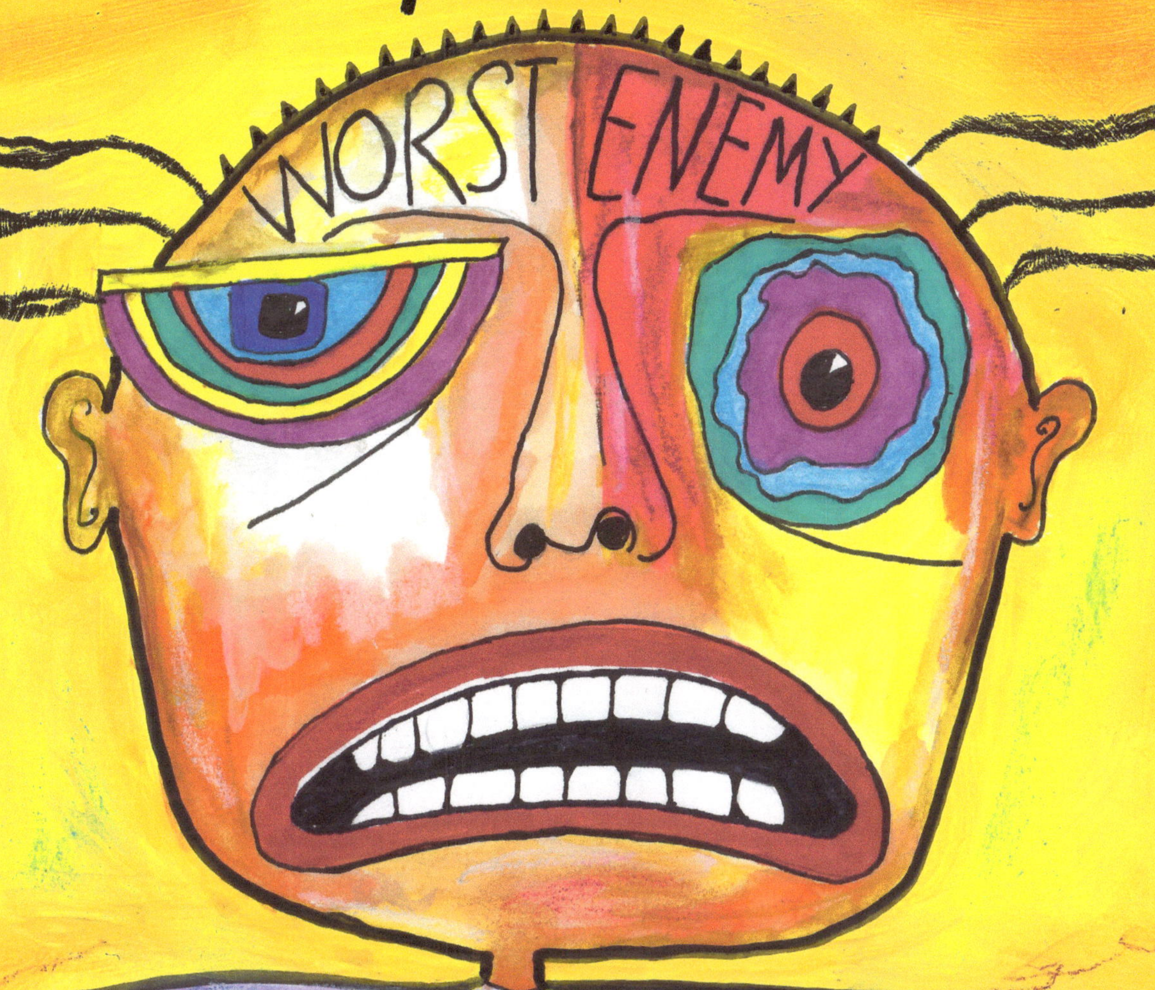

doesn't Live between Your own 2 ears.
~ Laird Hamilton

51

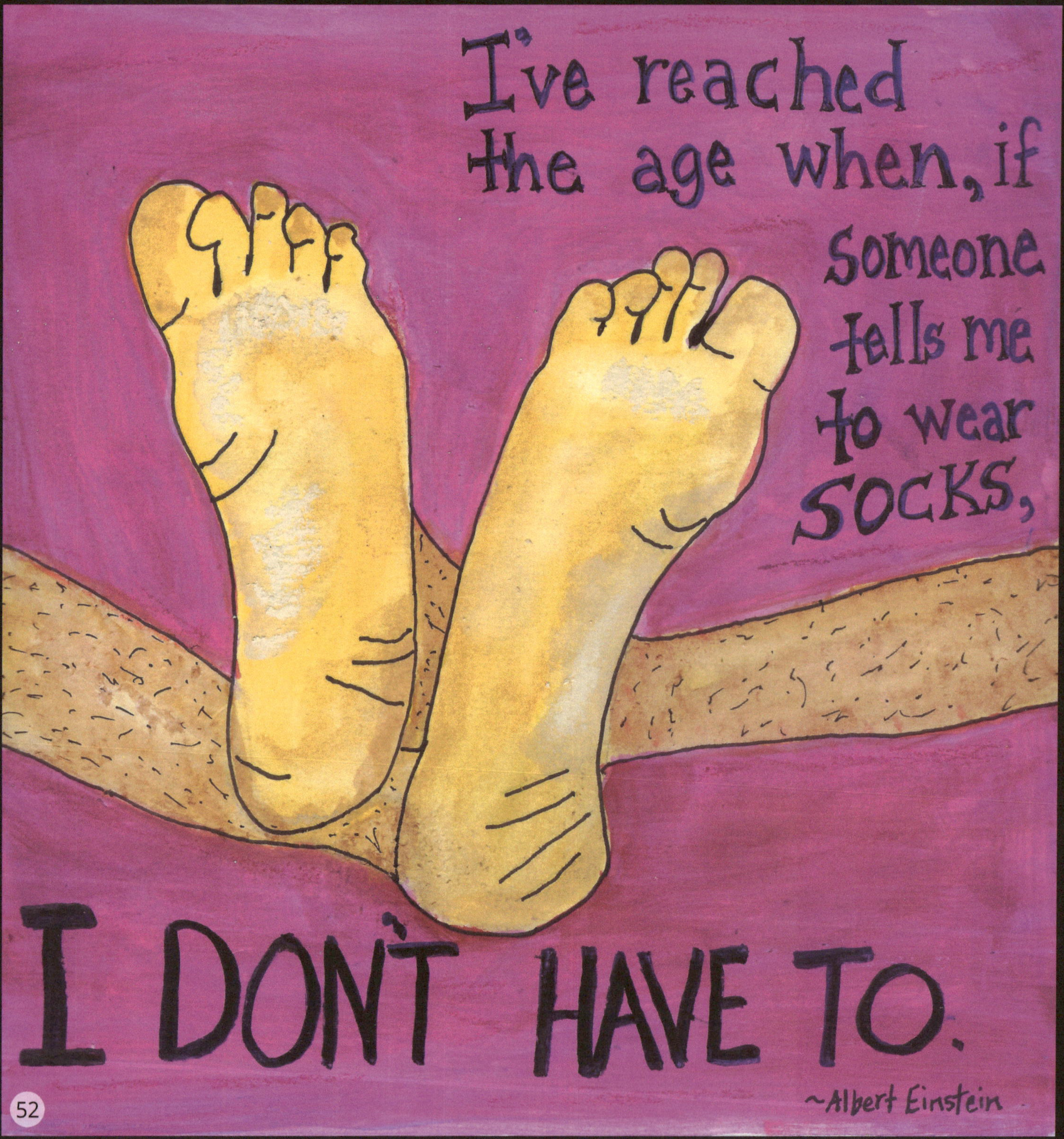

I've reached the age when, if someone tells me to wear socks,
I DON'T HAVE TO.
~Albert Einstein
52

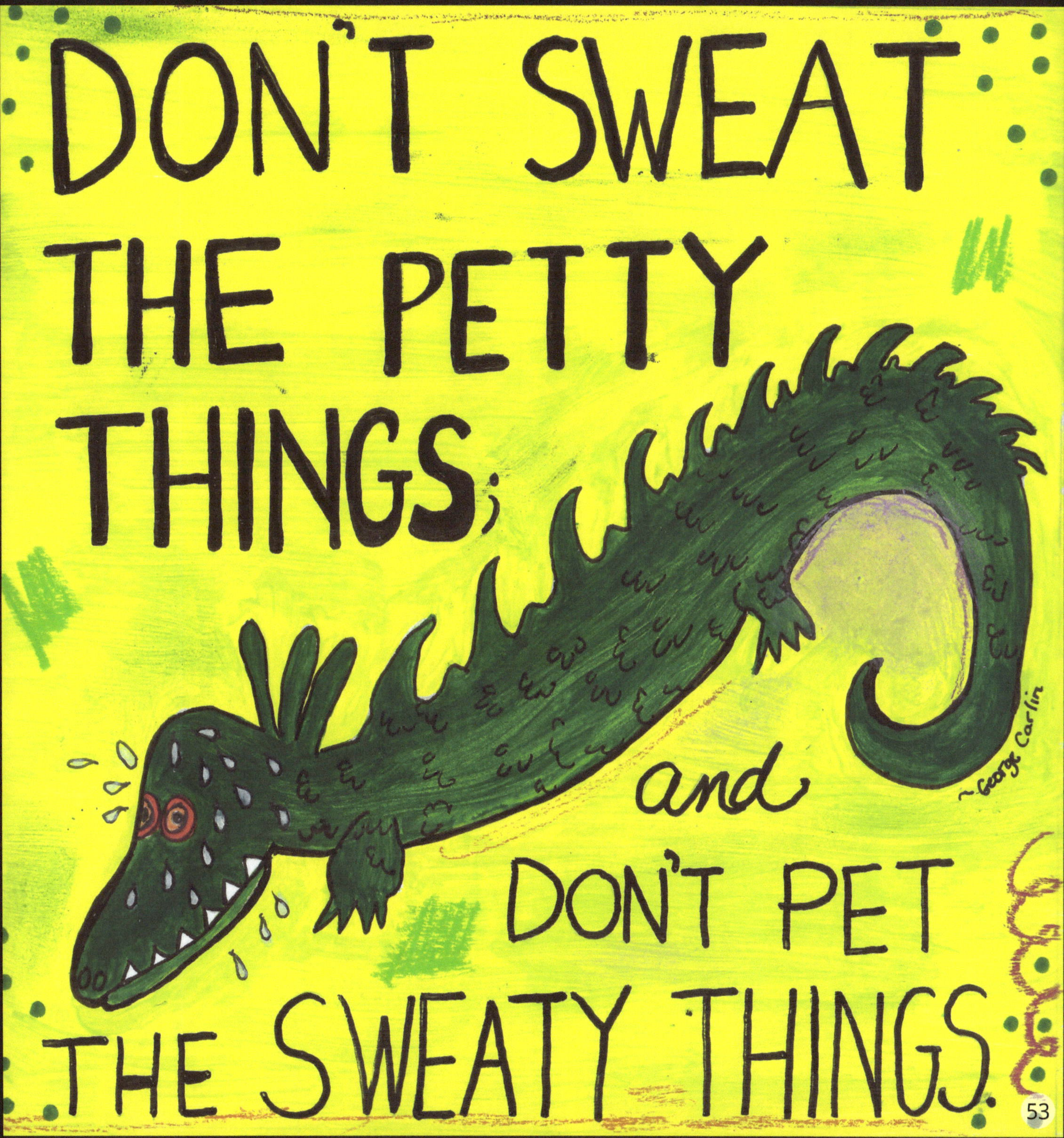

DON'T SWEAT
THE PETTY
THINGS;
and
DON'T PET
THE SWEATY THINGS.
~George Carlin
53

Hate has 4 letters, so does LOVE. Enemies has 7 letters, so does FRIENDS. Lying has 5 letters, so does TRUTH. NEGATIVE has 8 letters, so does POSITIVE. UNDER has 5, so does ABOVE. CRY has 3 letters, so does JOY. ANGER has 5 letters, so does HAPPY. RIGHT has 5 letters, so does WRONG. HURT has 4 letters, so does HEAL. Life can seem like a double-edged sword. Choose the positive ALWAYS.

54

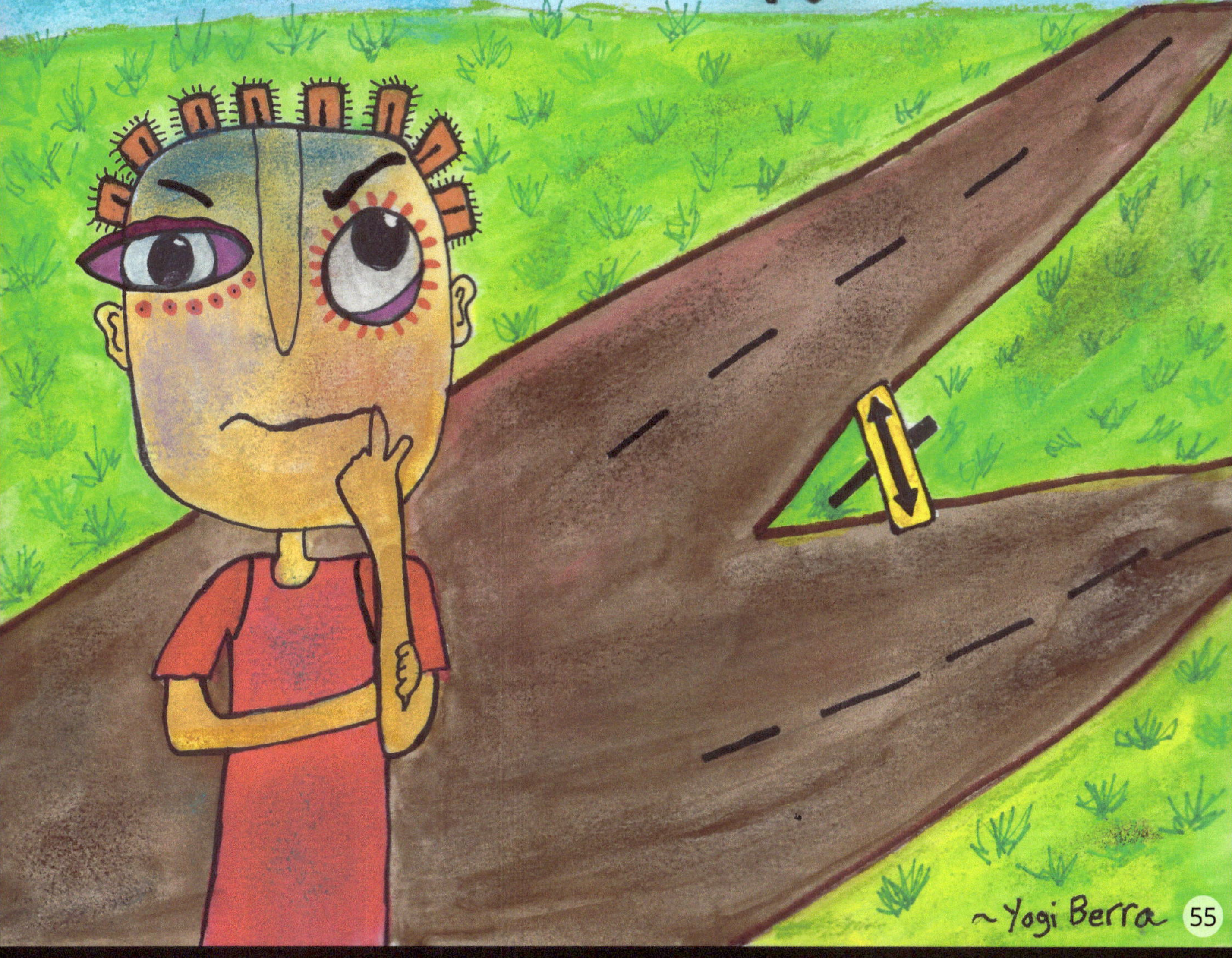

WHEN YOU COME TO A FORK IN THE ROAD, TAKE IT.
~Yogi Berra
55

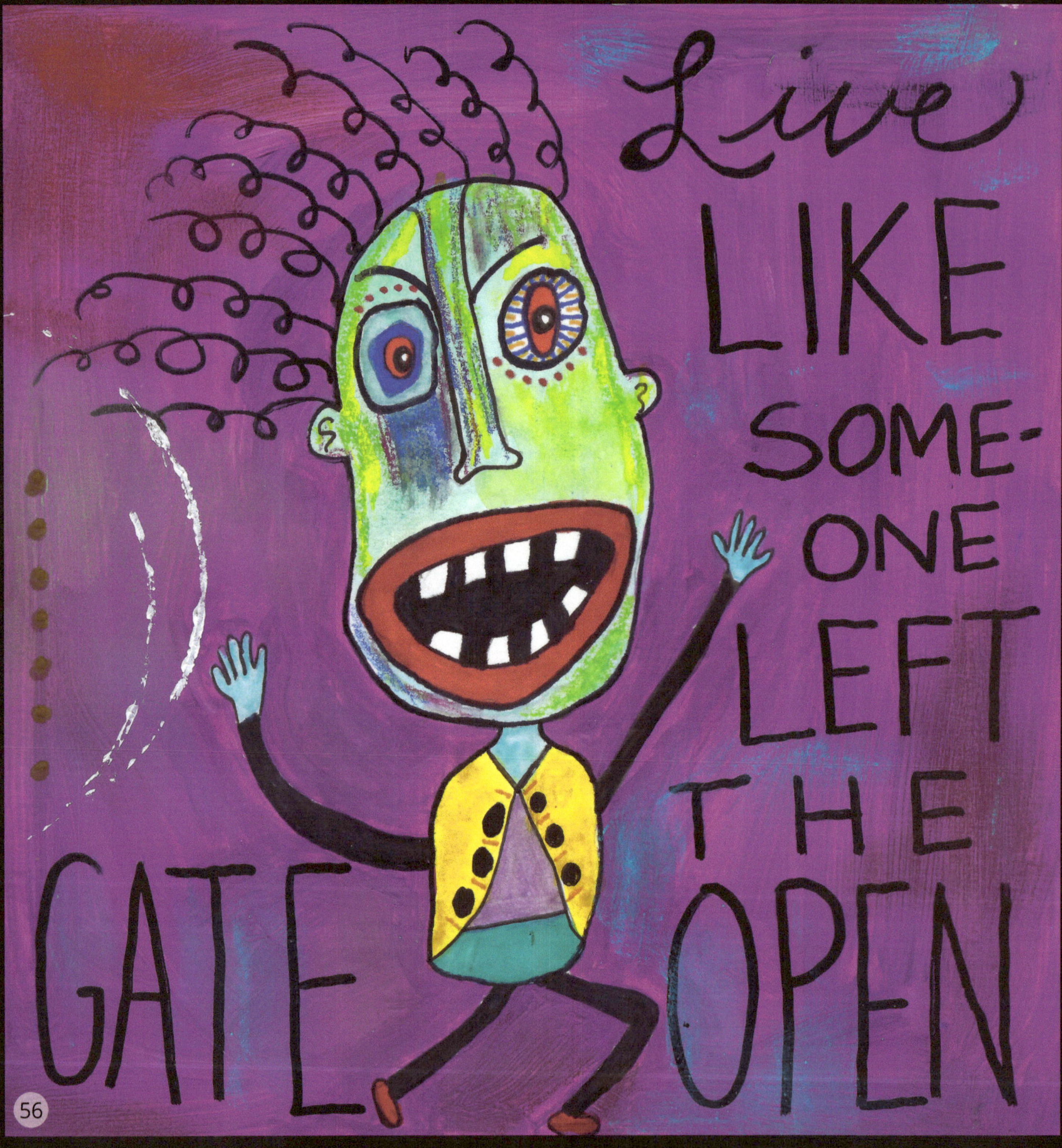

Live
LIKE
SOME-
ONE
LEFT
THE
OPEN
GATE

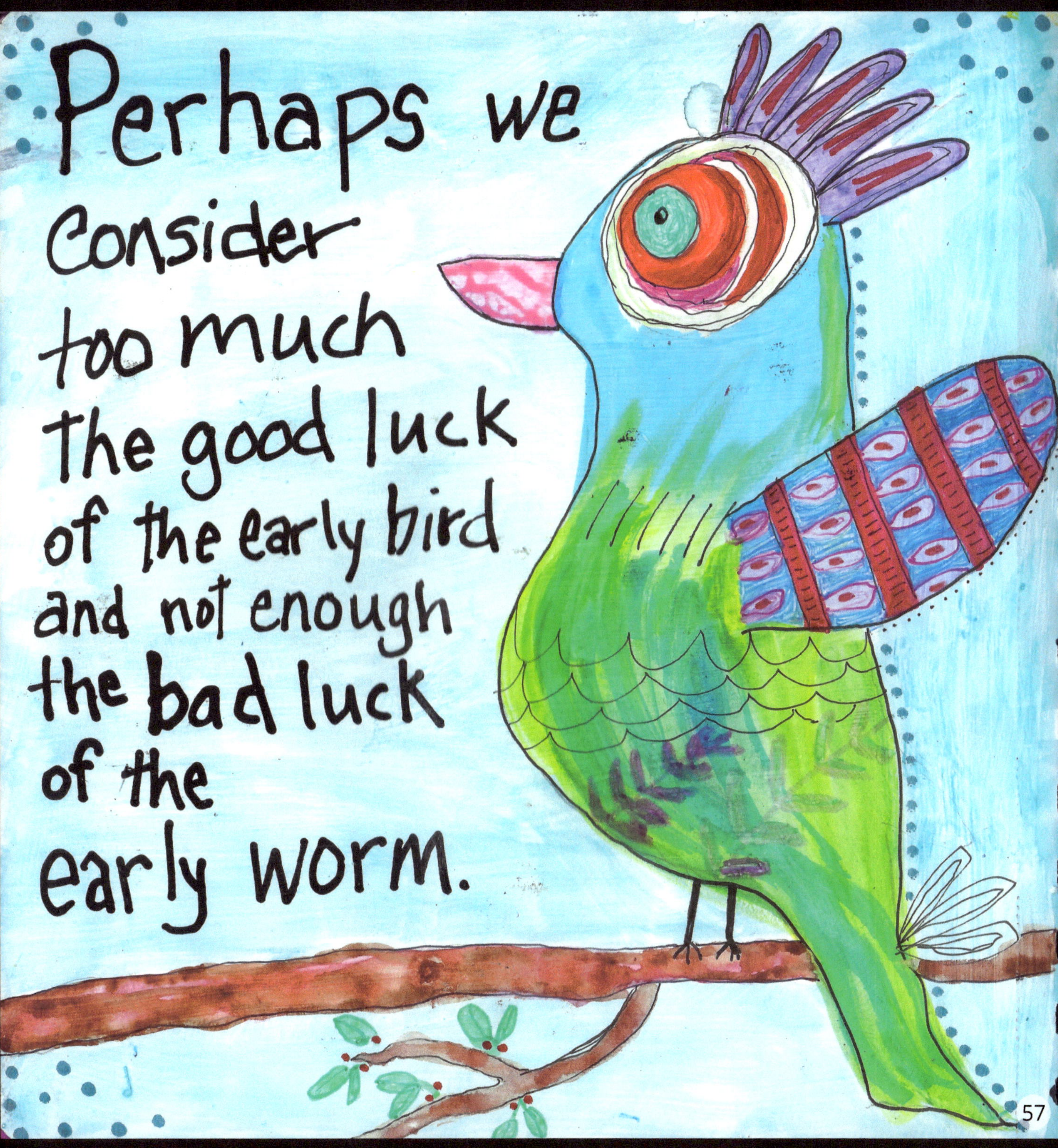

Perhaps we consider too much the good luck of the early bird and not enough the bad luck of the early worm.

FRIENDSHIP
is like
Peeing in your pants.

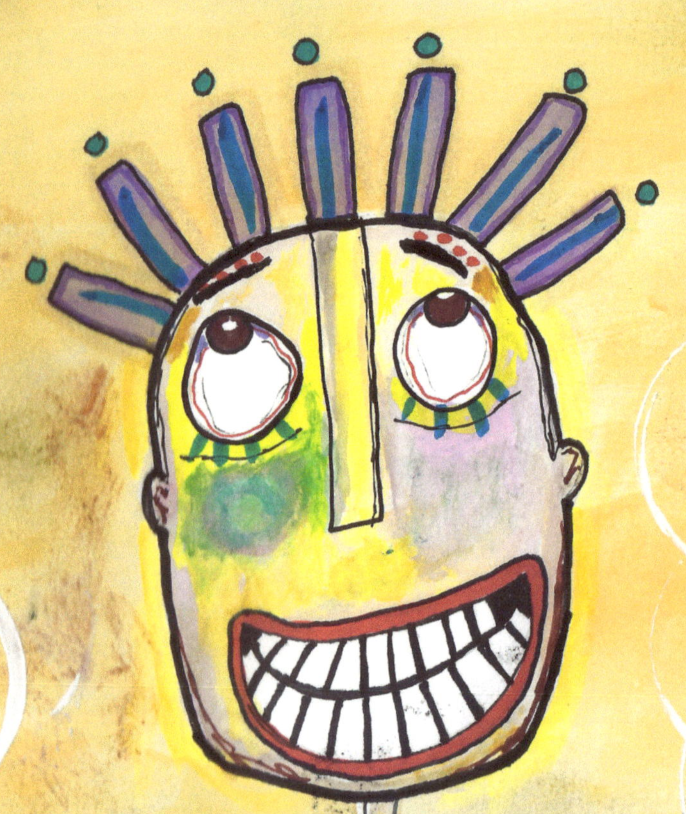

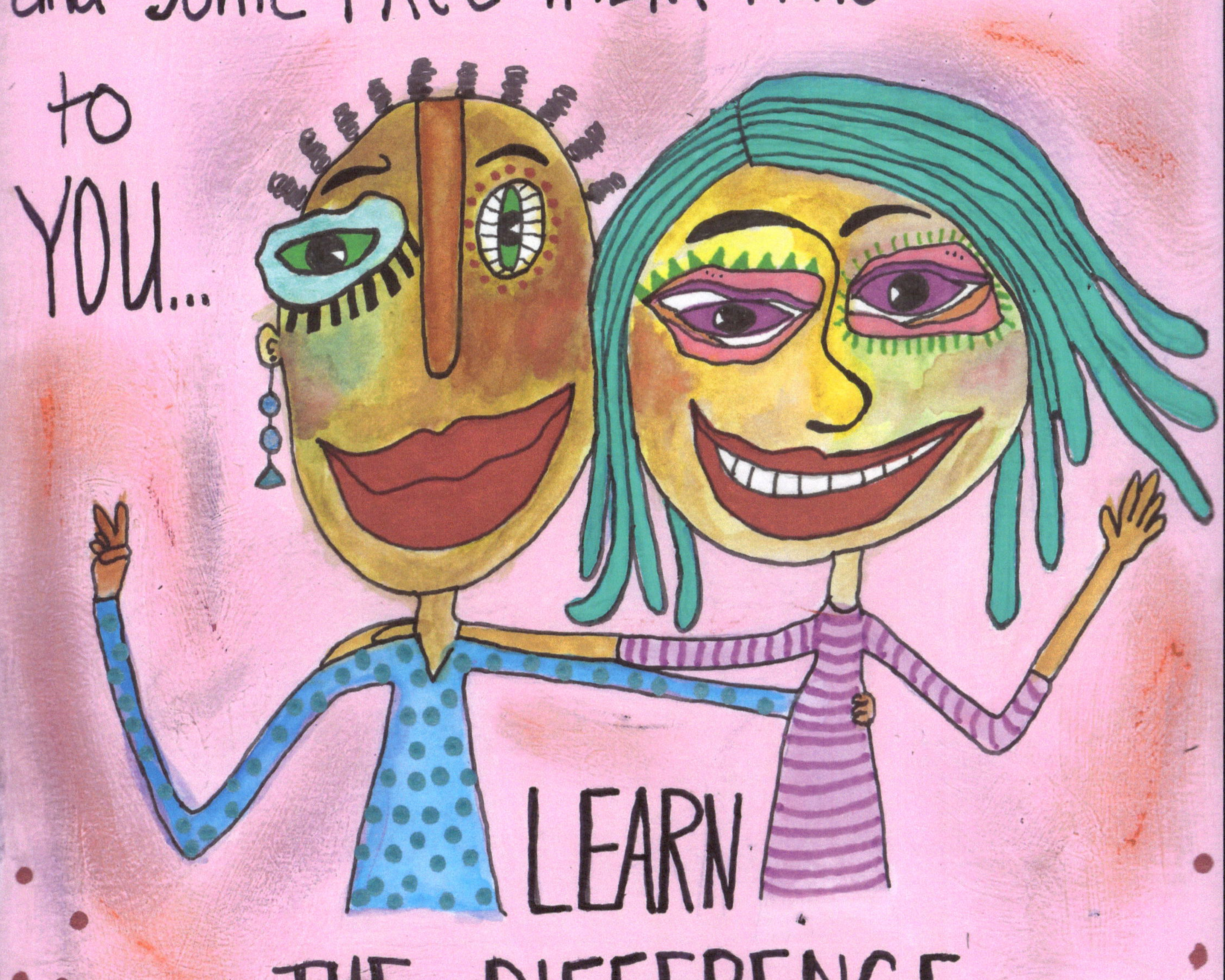

Some talk to you in their FREE time
and some FREE THEIR time to talk
to YOU...
LEARN
THE DIFFERENCE
59

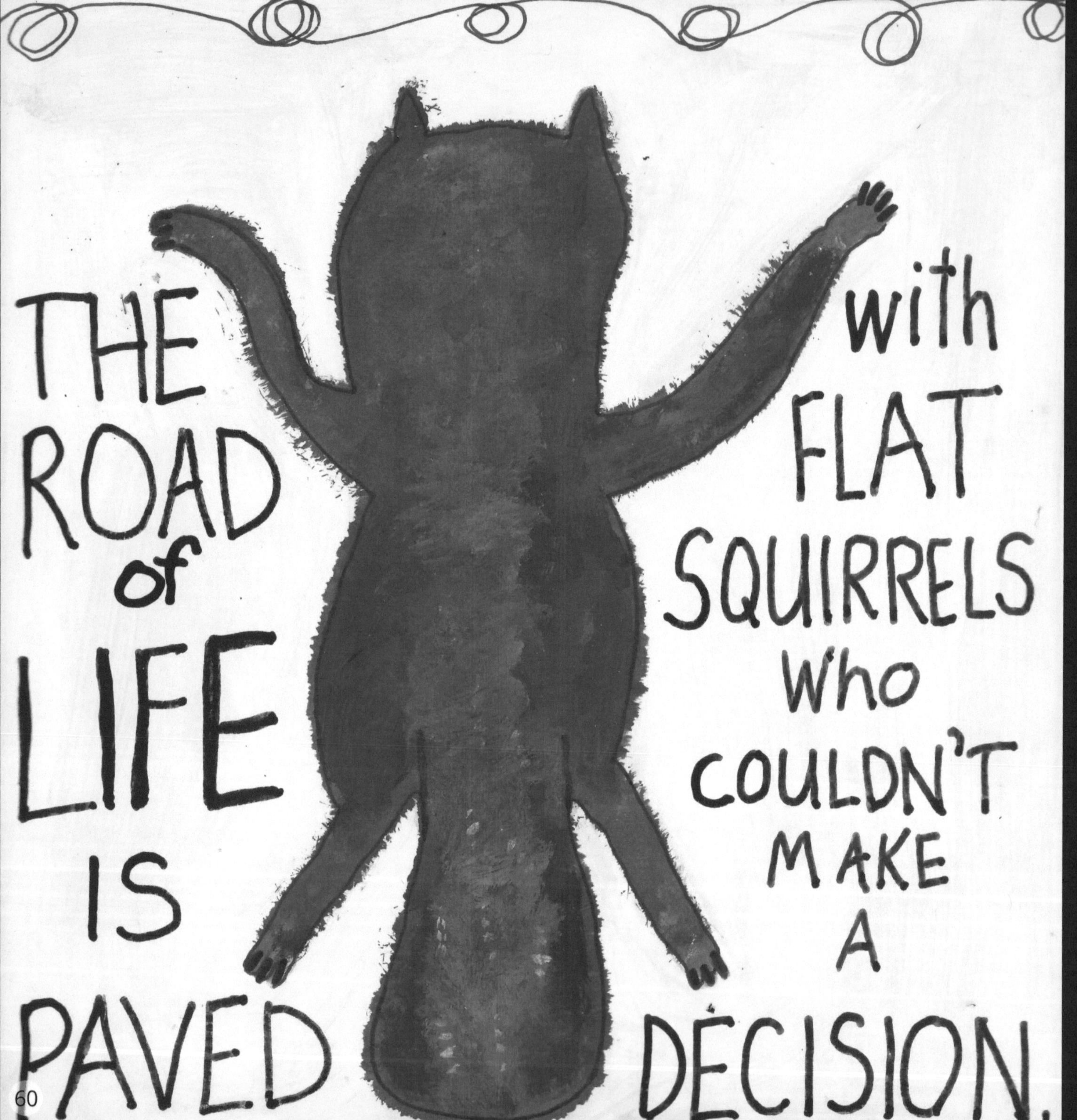

THE ROAD of LIFE IS PAVED
with FLAT SQUIRRELS Who COULDN'T MAKE A DECISION.

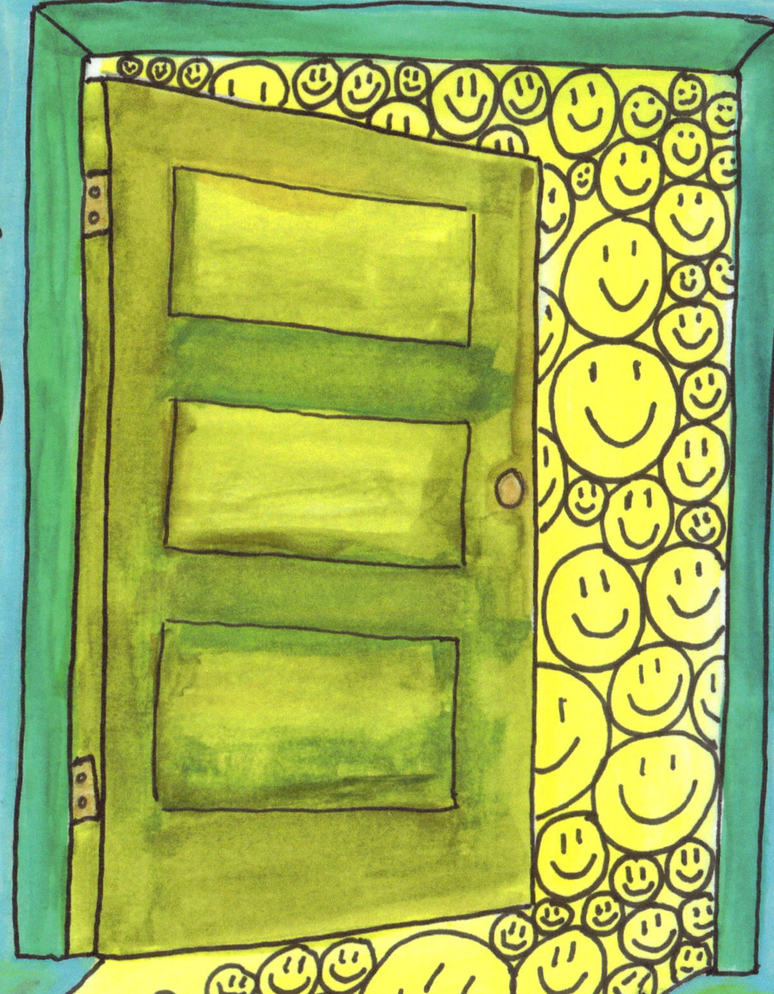

HAPPINESS
OFTEN SNEAKS THROUGH A DOOR
YOU didn't KNOW YOU LEFT OPEN.
~John Barrymore

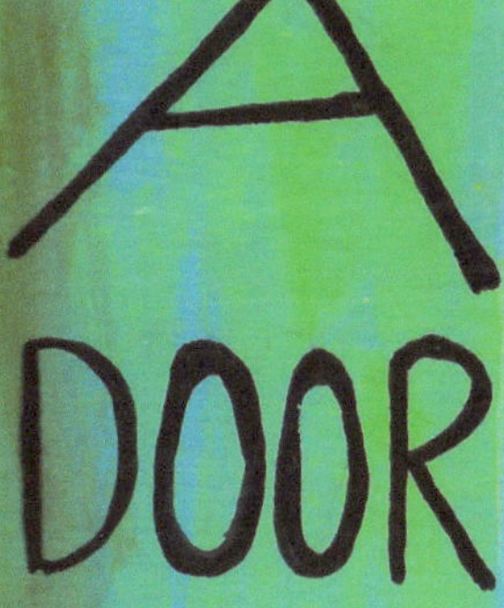

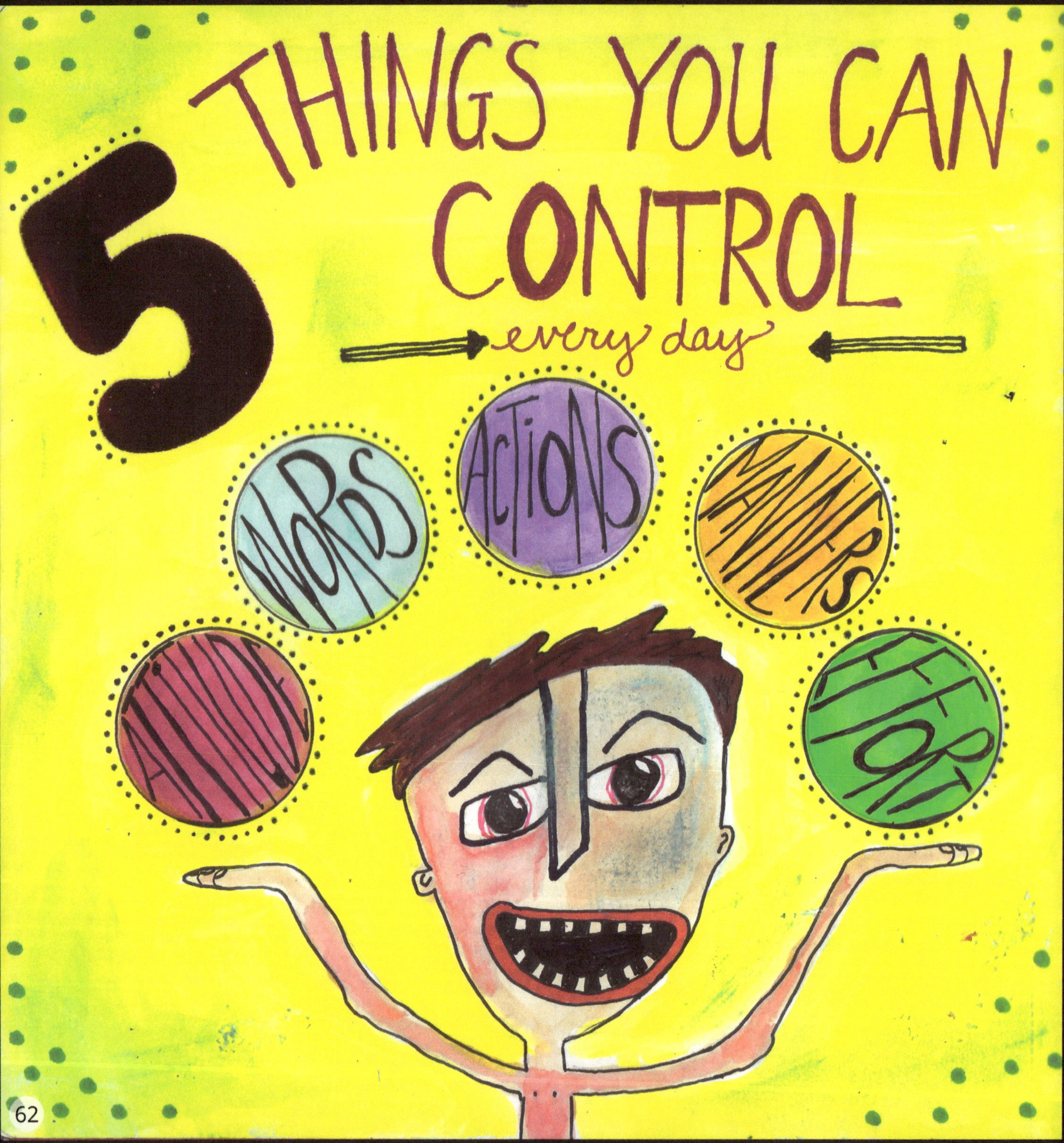

5
THINGS YOU CAN
CONTROL
every day
WORDS
ACTIONS
MANNERS
ATTITUDE
EFFORT

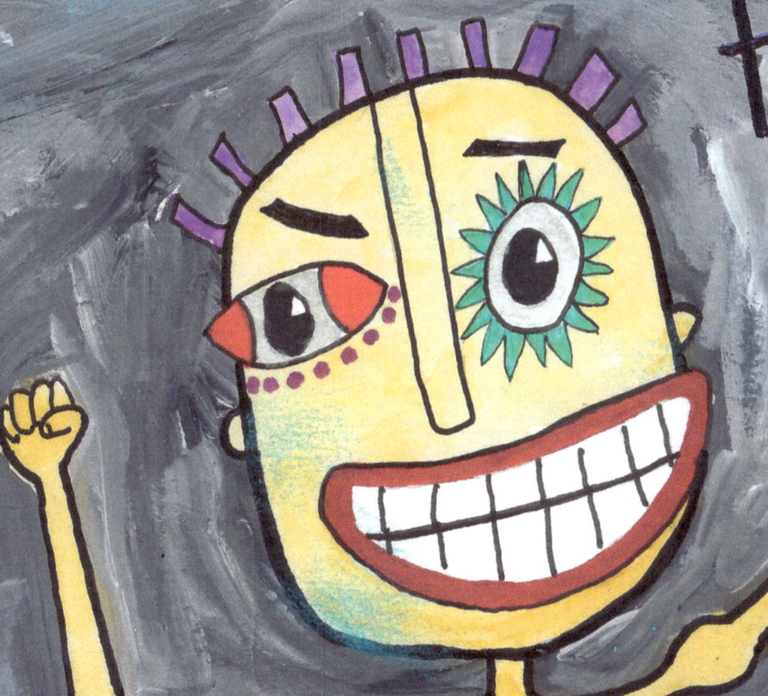

Never Trust Your fears...
They don't Know your strength.
ATHENA SINGH
63

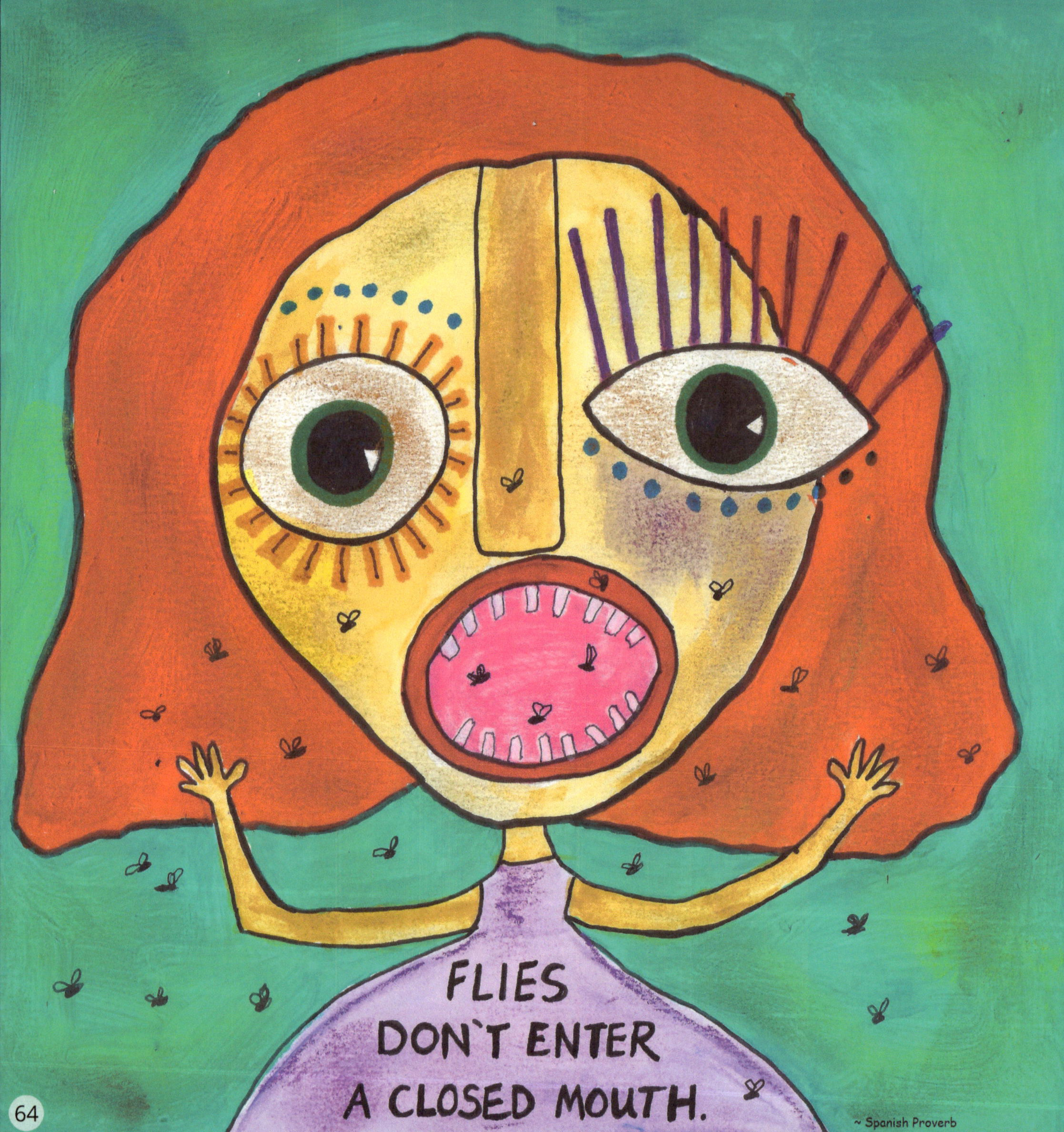

FLIES
DON'T ENTER
A CLOSED MOUTH.
~ Spanish Proverb

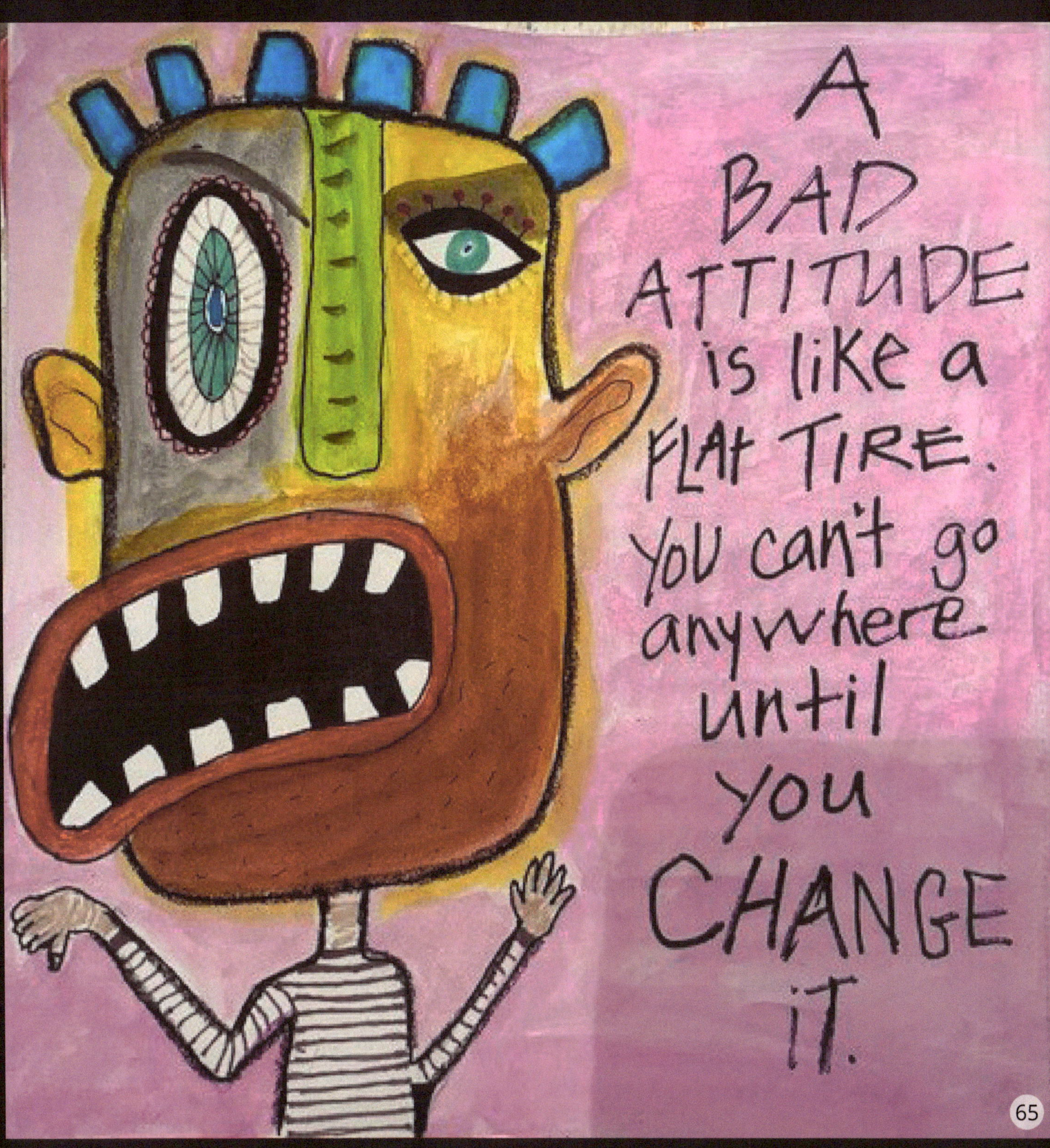
A BAD ATTITUDE is like a FLAt TIRE. You can't go anywhere until you CHANGE it.

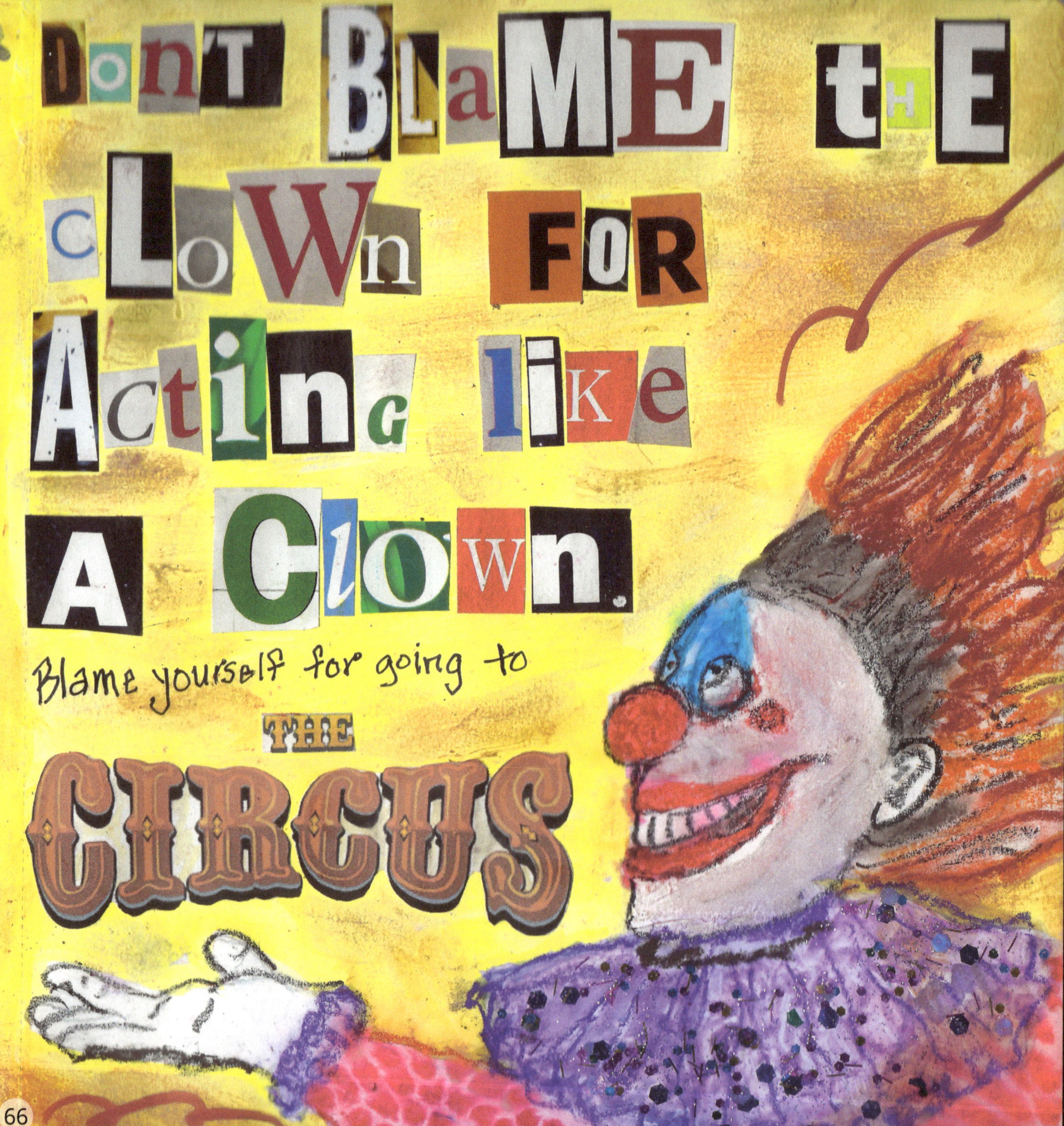

DoN'T BLaME thE
CLoWn FOR
Acting like
A CLown.
Blame yourself for going to
THE
CIRCUS

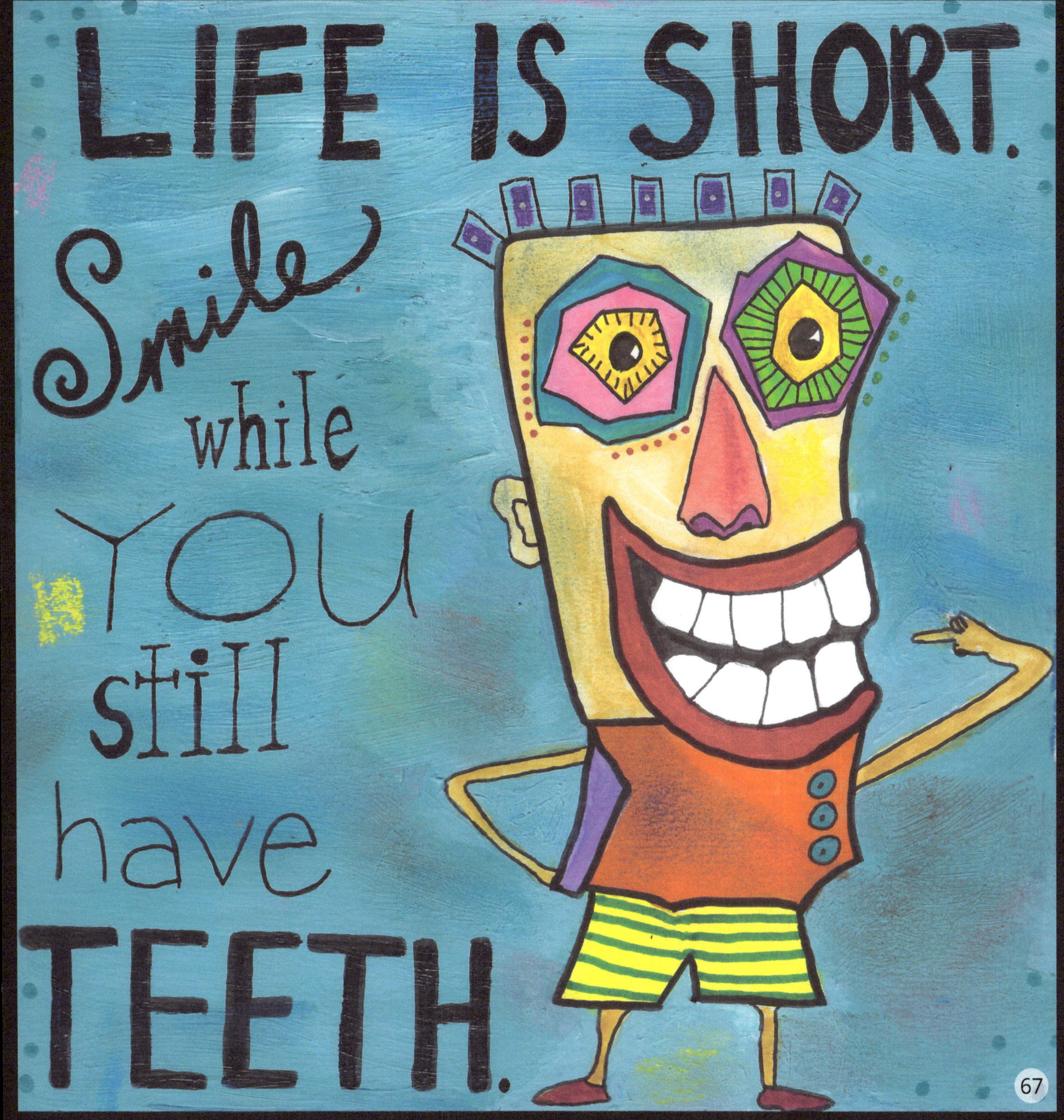

LIFE IS SHORT.
Smile while YOU still have TEETH.
67

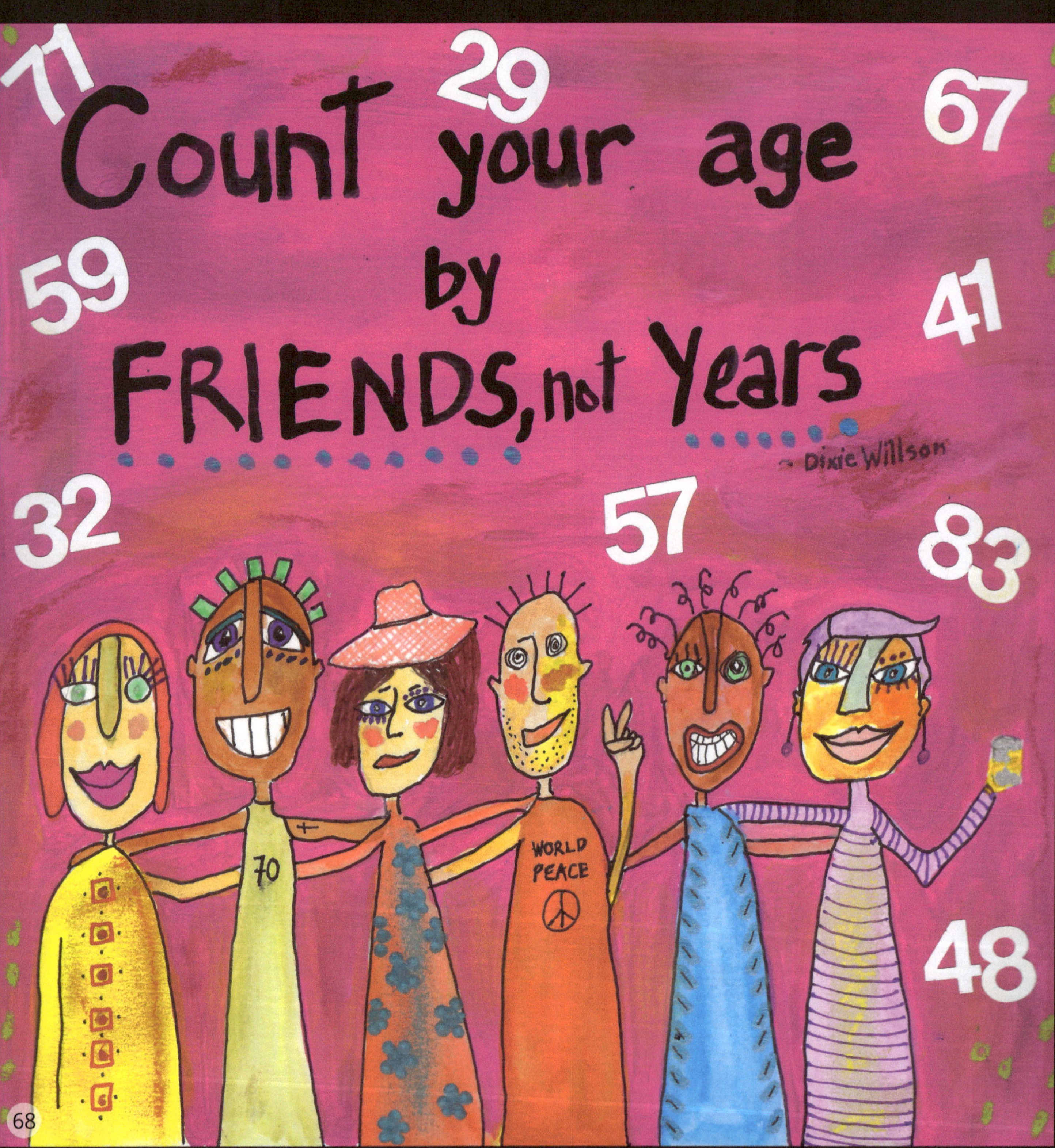
71
29
67
Count your age
by
FRIENDS, not Years
~ Dixie Willson
59
41
32
57
83
70
WORLD
PEACE
48
68

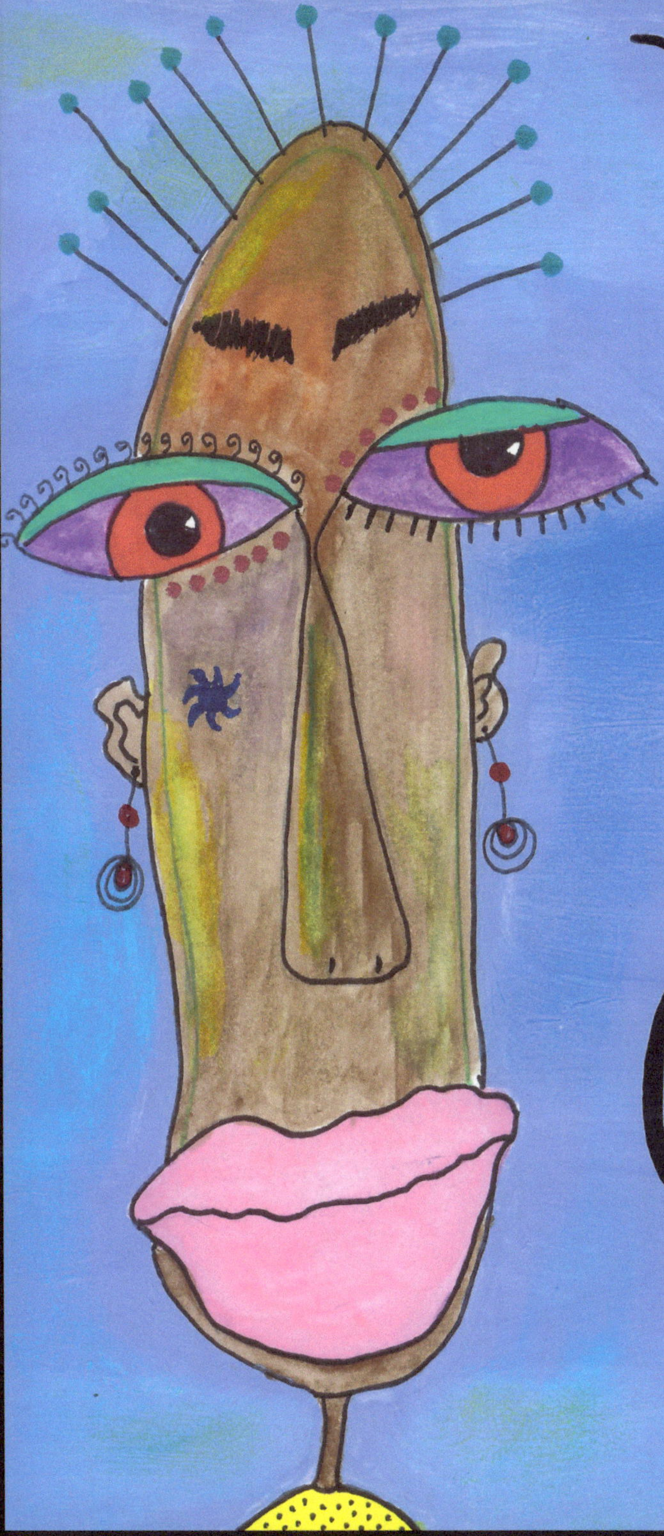

Whatever
YOU ARE,
be a
GOOD
ONE.
~Abraham Lincoln

WHEN YOU LEARN HOW MUCH YOU'RE WORTH,

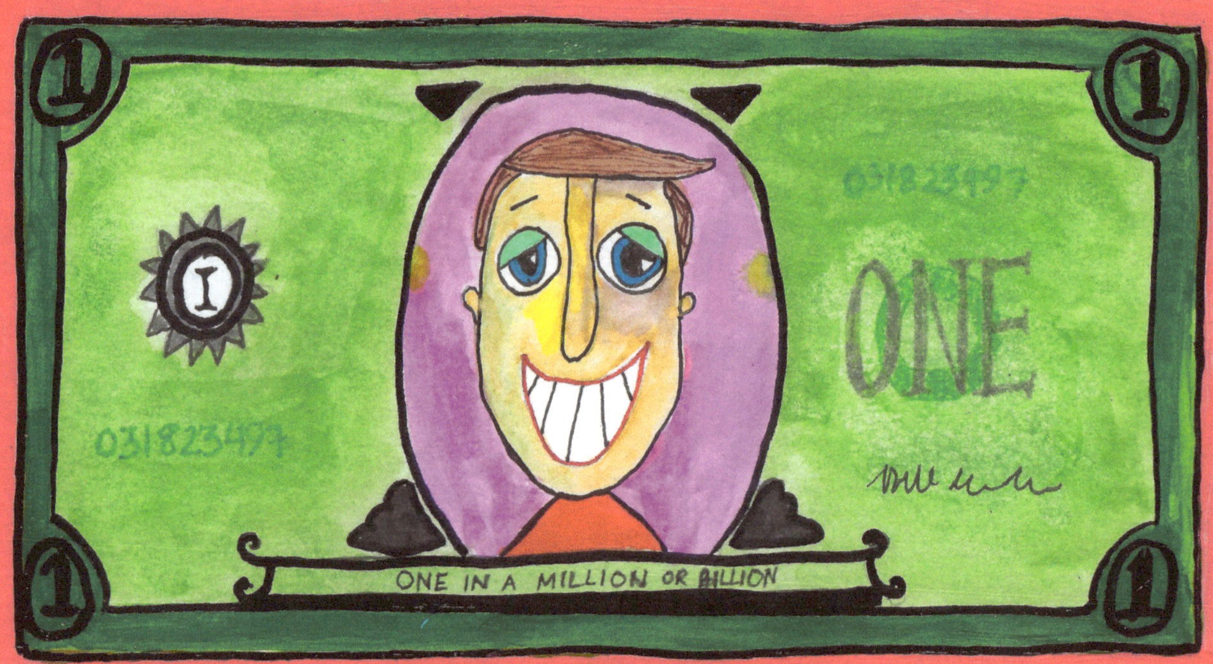

YOU'LL STOP GIVING PEOPLE DISCOUNTS

~ Karen Salmansohn

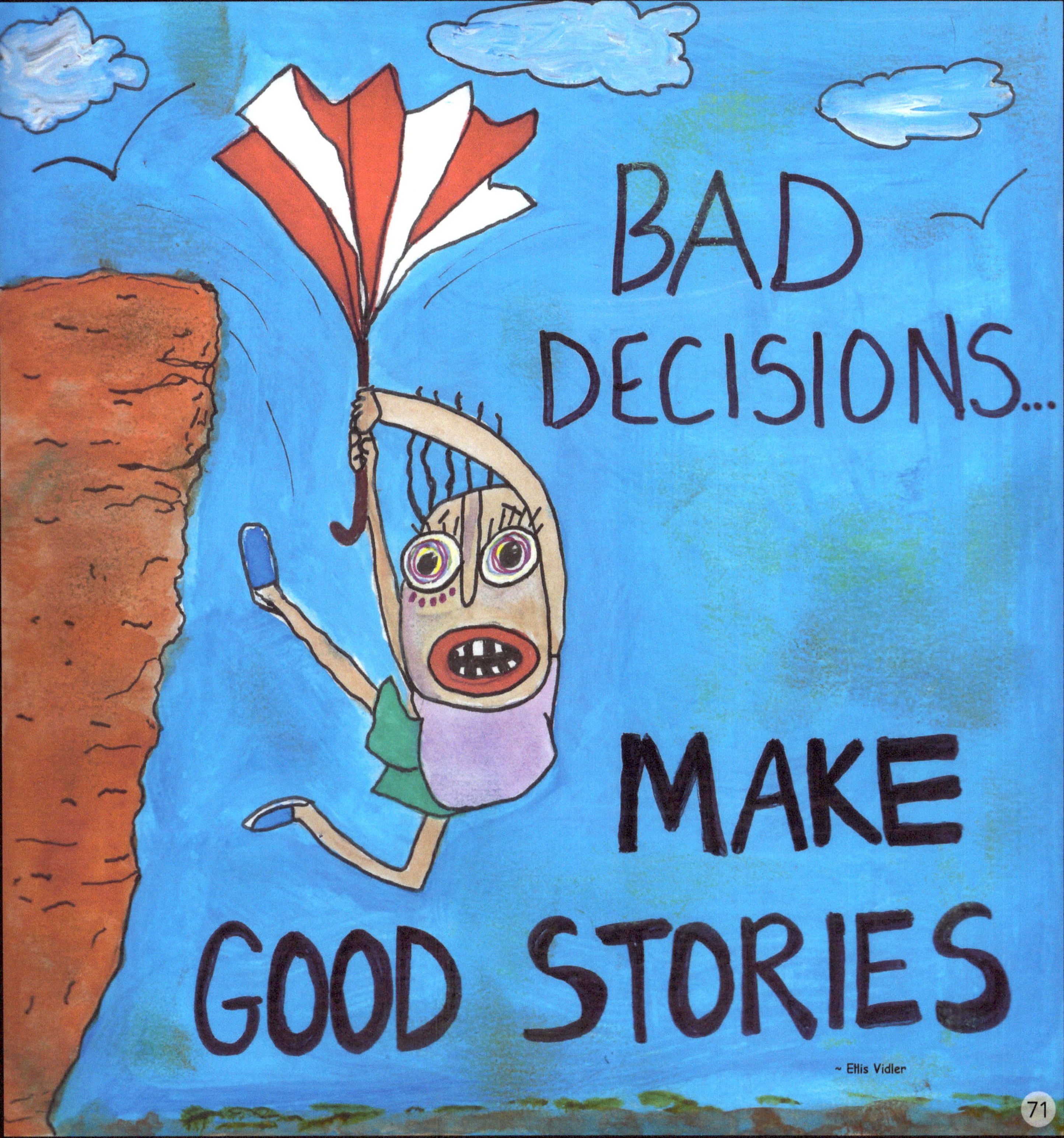

BAD DECISIONS...
MAKE
GOOD STORIES
~ Ellis Vidler

YESTERDAY
Today
DON'T LET YESTERDAY TAKE UP TOO MUCH OF TODAY. ~ WILL ROGERS

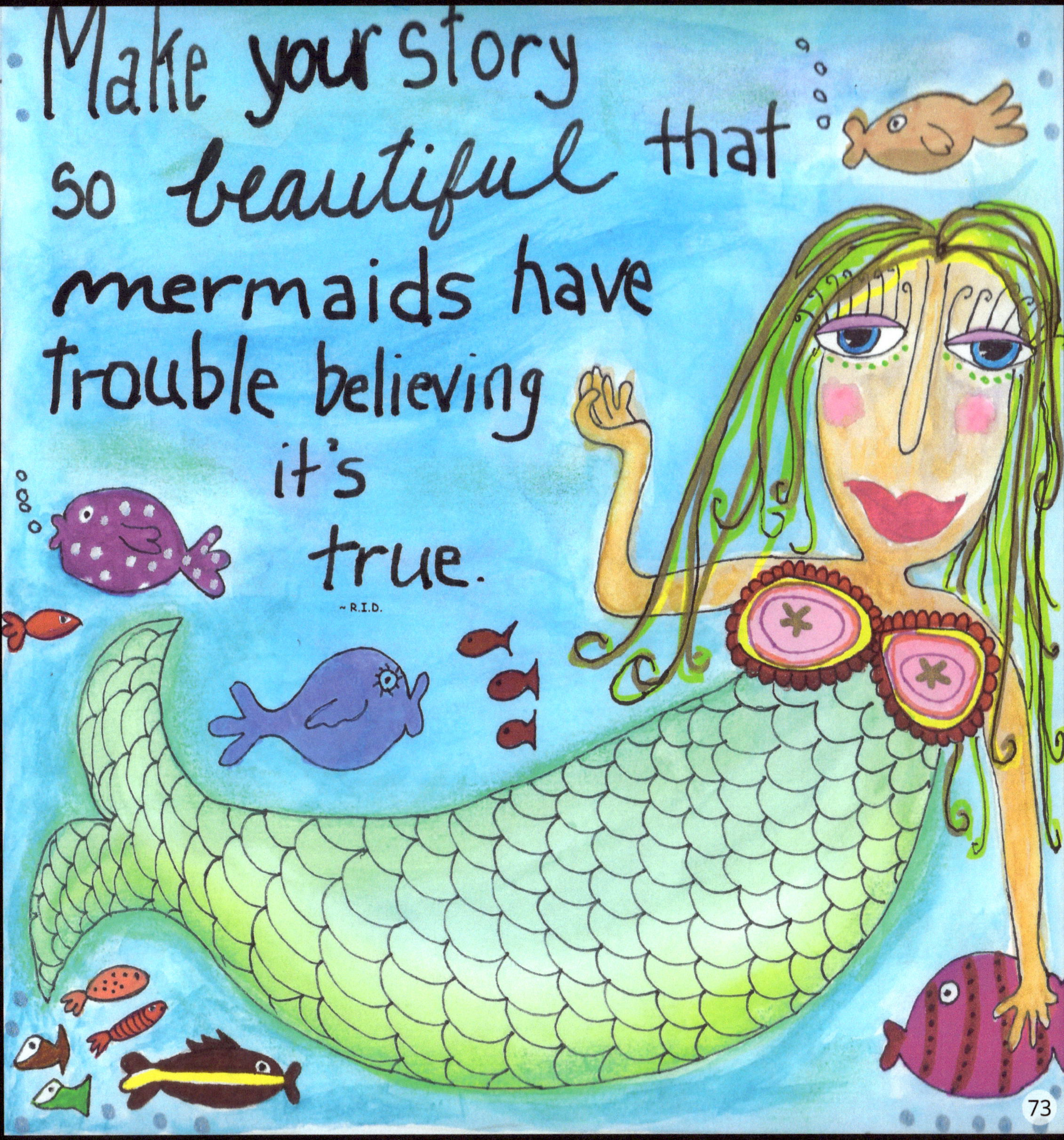

Make your story so *beautiful* that mermaids have trouble believing it's true.

~ R.I.D.

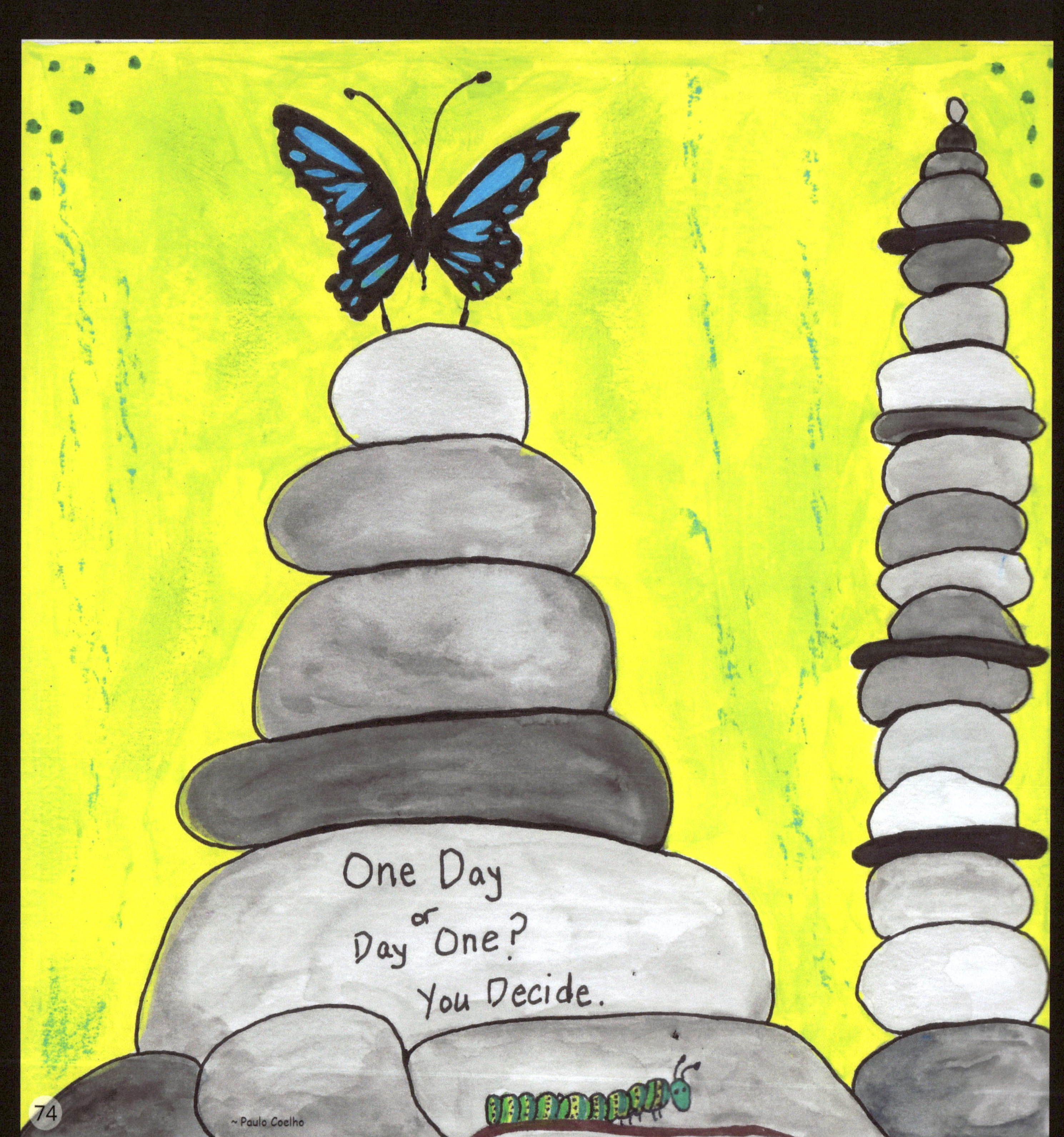

One Day
or
Day One?
You Decide.
~ Paulo Coelho

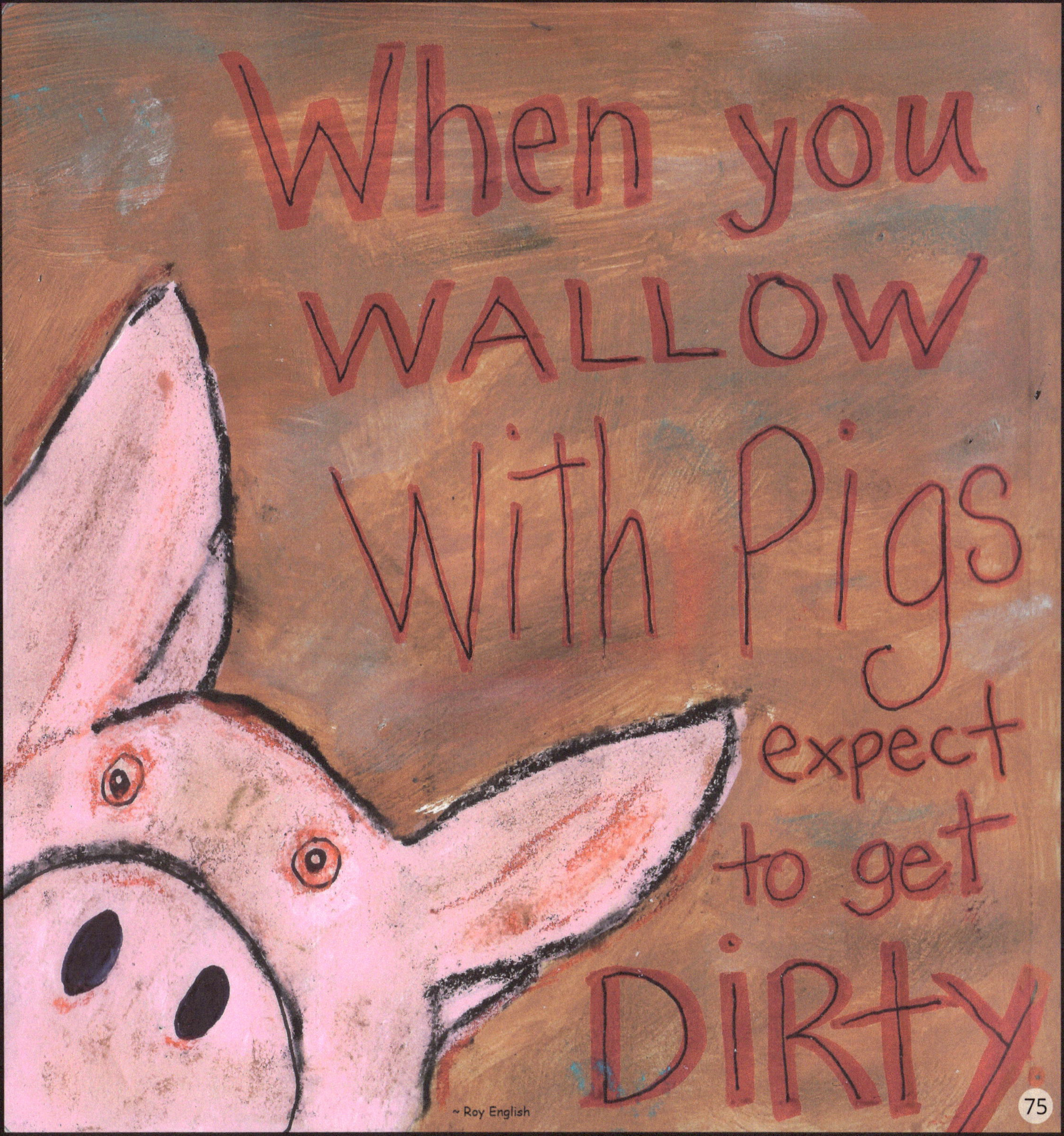

When you
wallow
with Pigs
expect
to get
DiRty.
~ Roy English
75

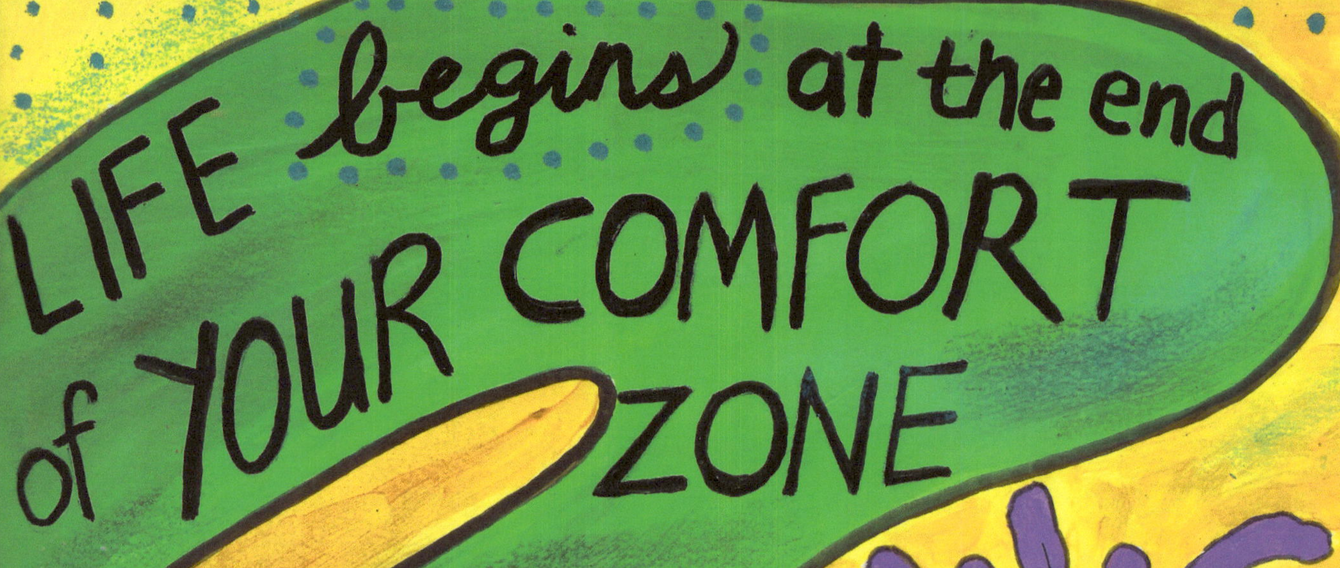

LIFE begins at the end of YOUR COMFORT ZONE
YOU ARE LEAVING YOUR COMFORT ZONE
WELCOME TO THE UNKNOWN
~ Neal Donald Walsh

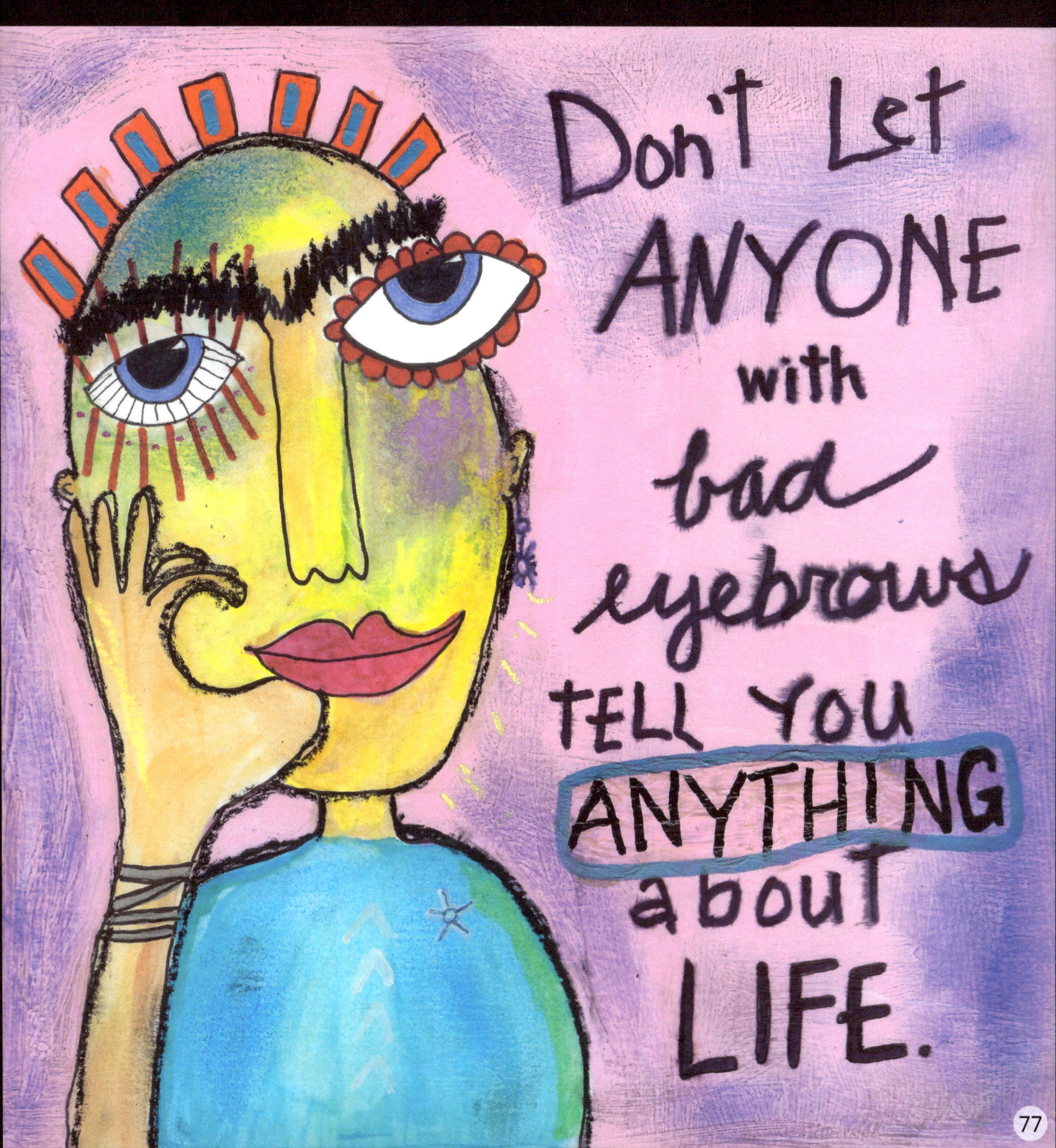
Don't Let ANYONE with bad eyebrows TELL YOU ANYTHING about LIFE.

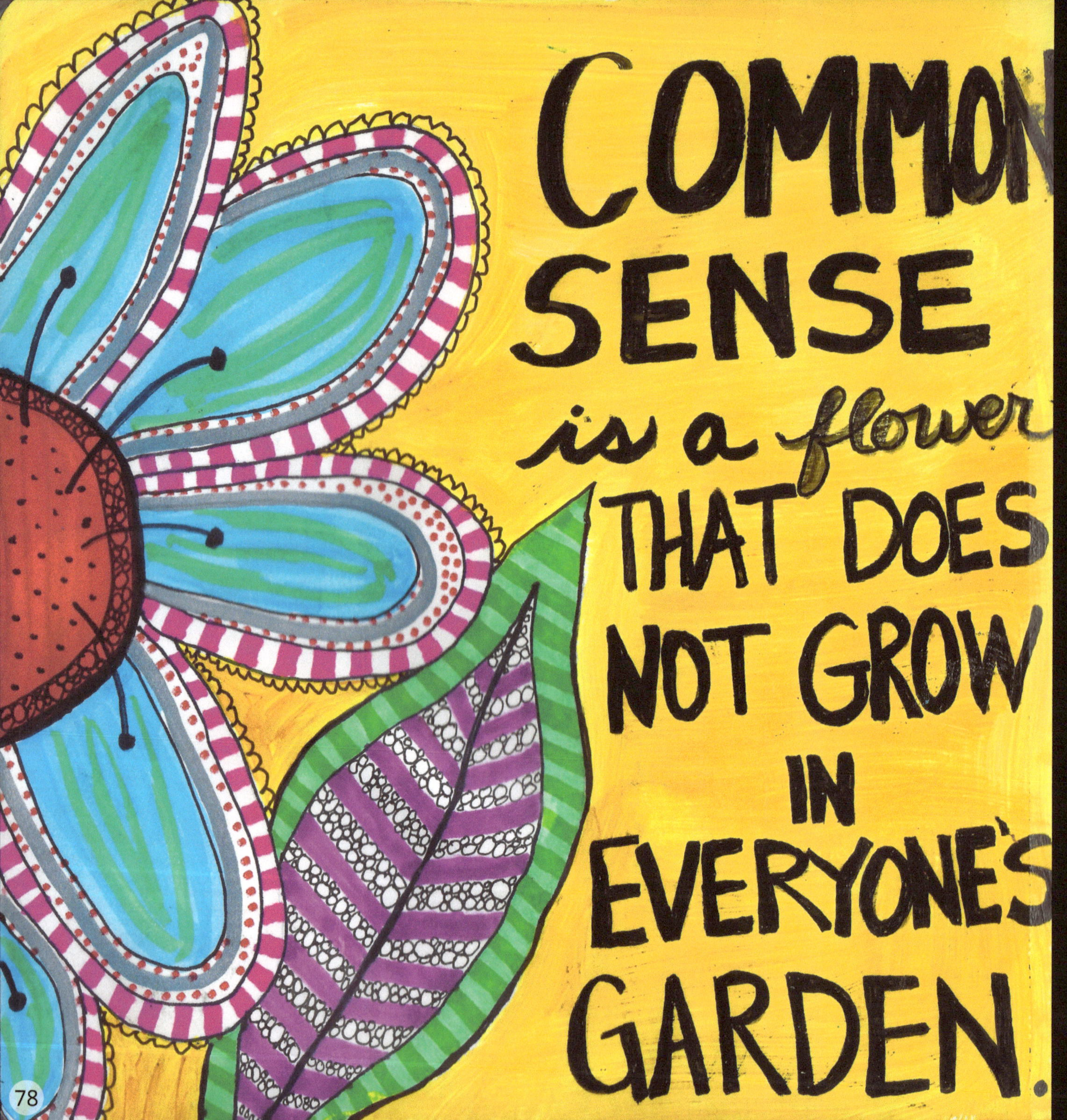
COMMON SENSE
is a flower
THAT DOES
NOT GROW
IN
EVERYONE'S
GARDEN.
78

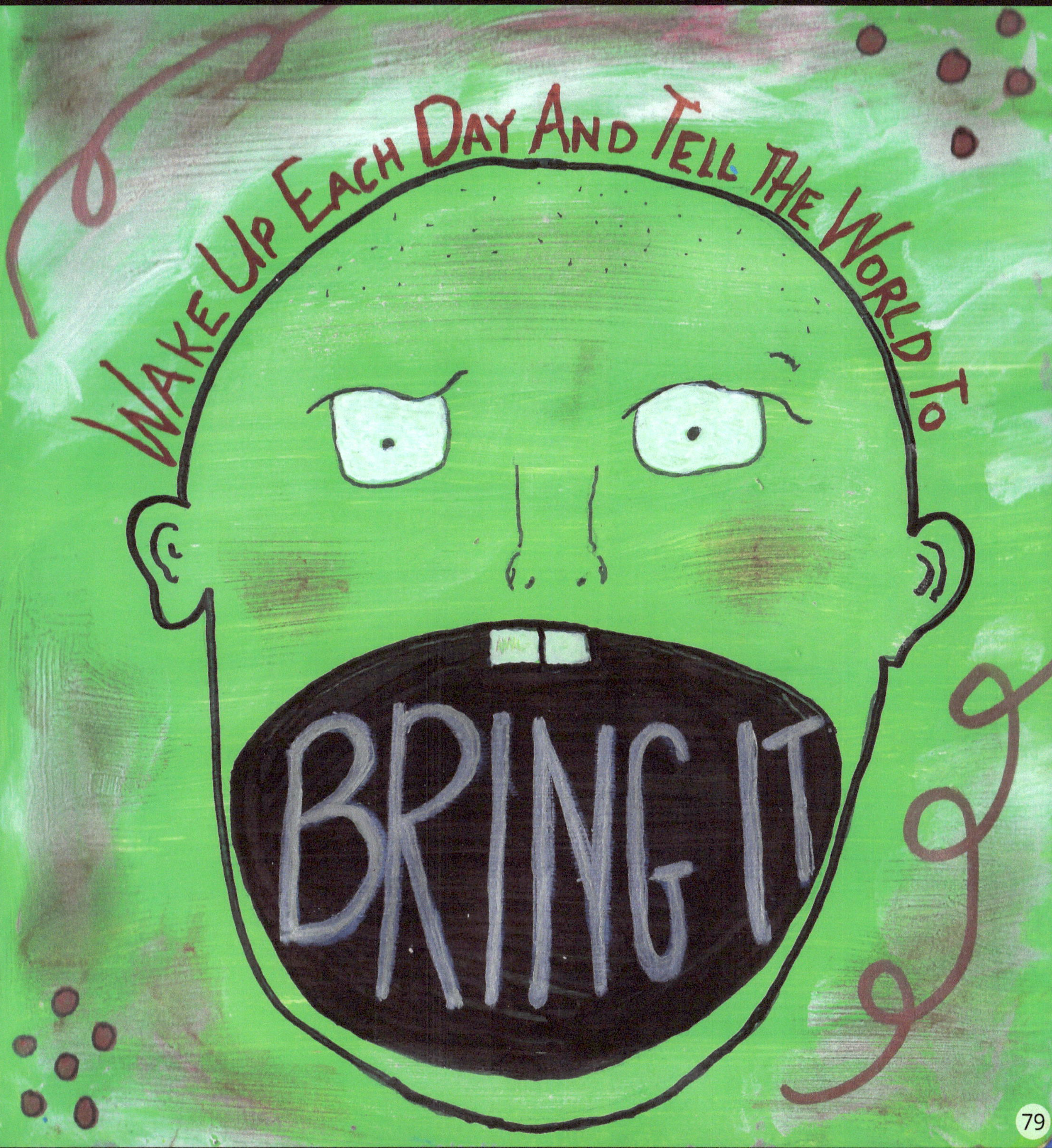

Wake Up Each Day And Tell The World To
BRING IT

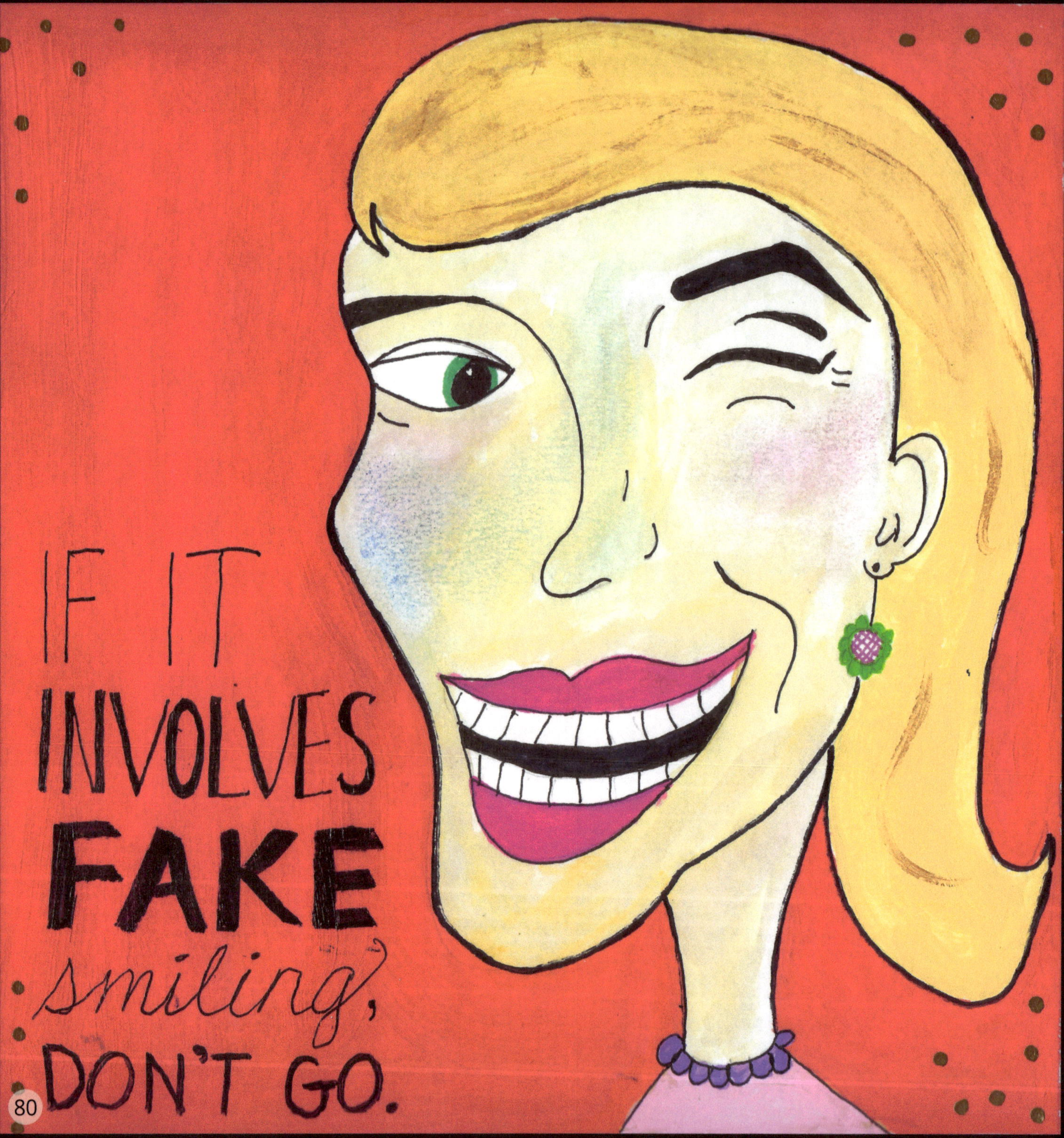

IF IT
INVOLVES
FAKE
smiling,
DON'T GO.

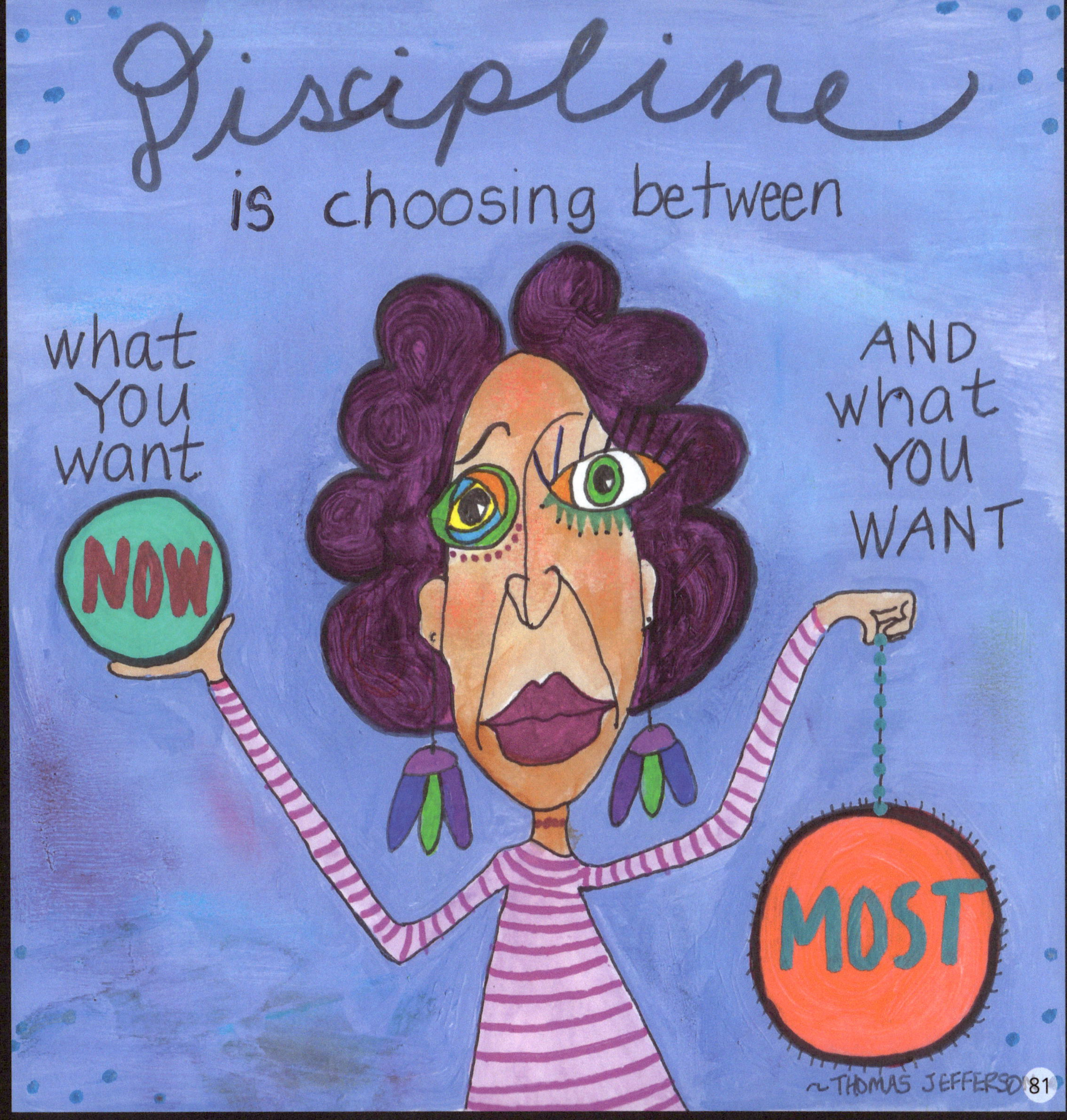

Discipline
is choosing between
what YOU want
AND what YOU WANT
NOW
MOST
~THOMAS JEFFERSON

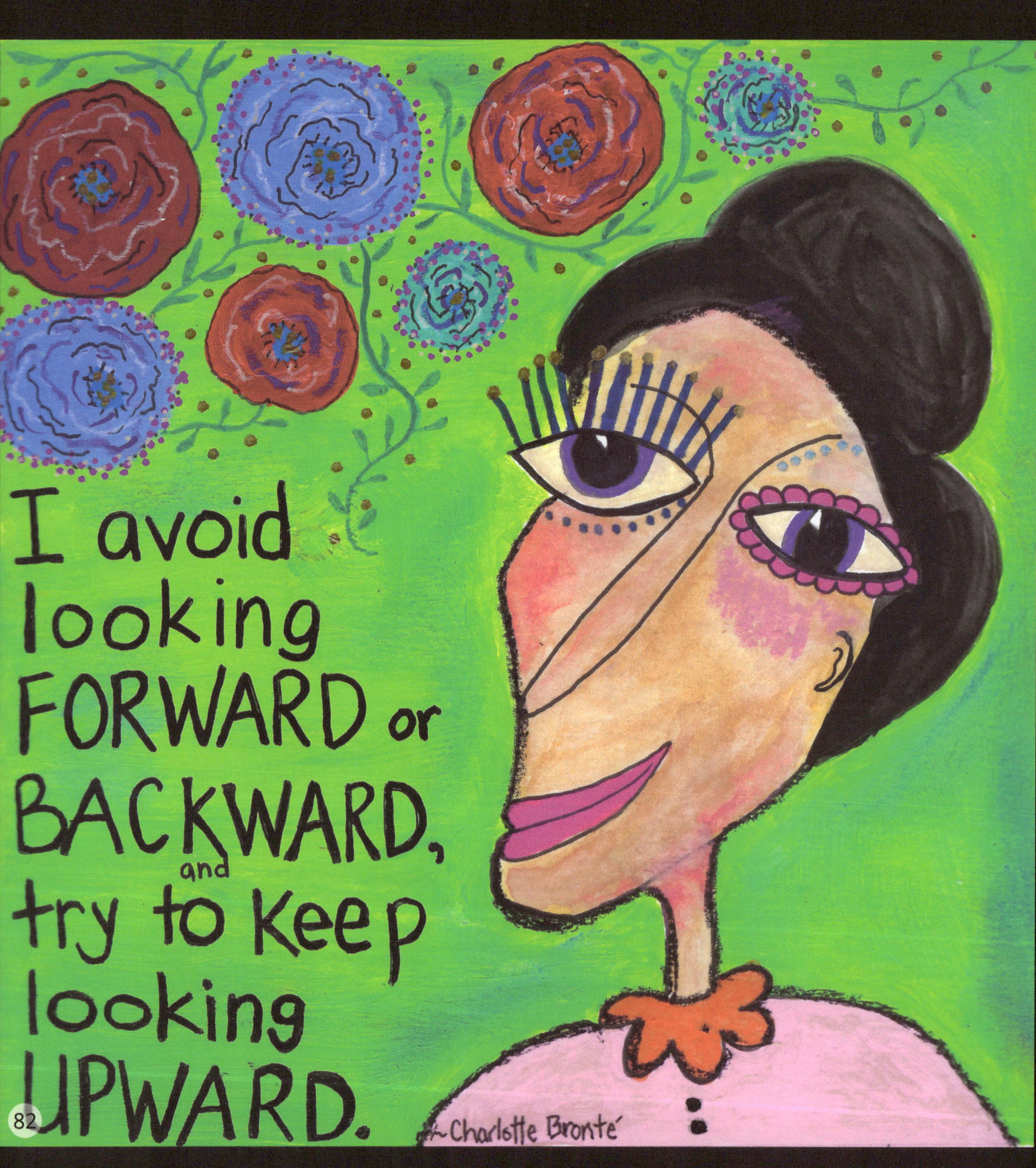

I avoid looking FORWARD or BACKWARD, and try to keep looking UPWARD.
~Charlotte Bronté
82

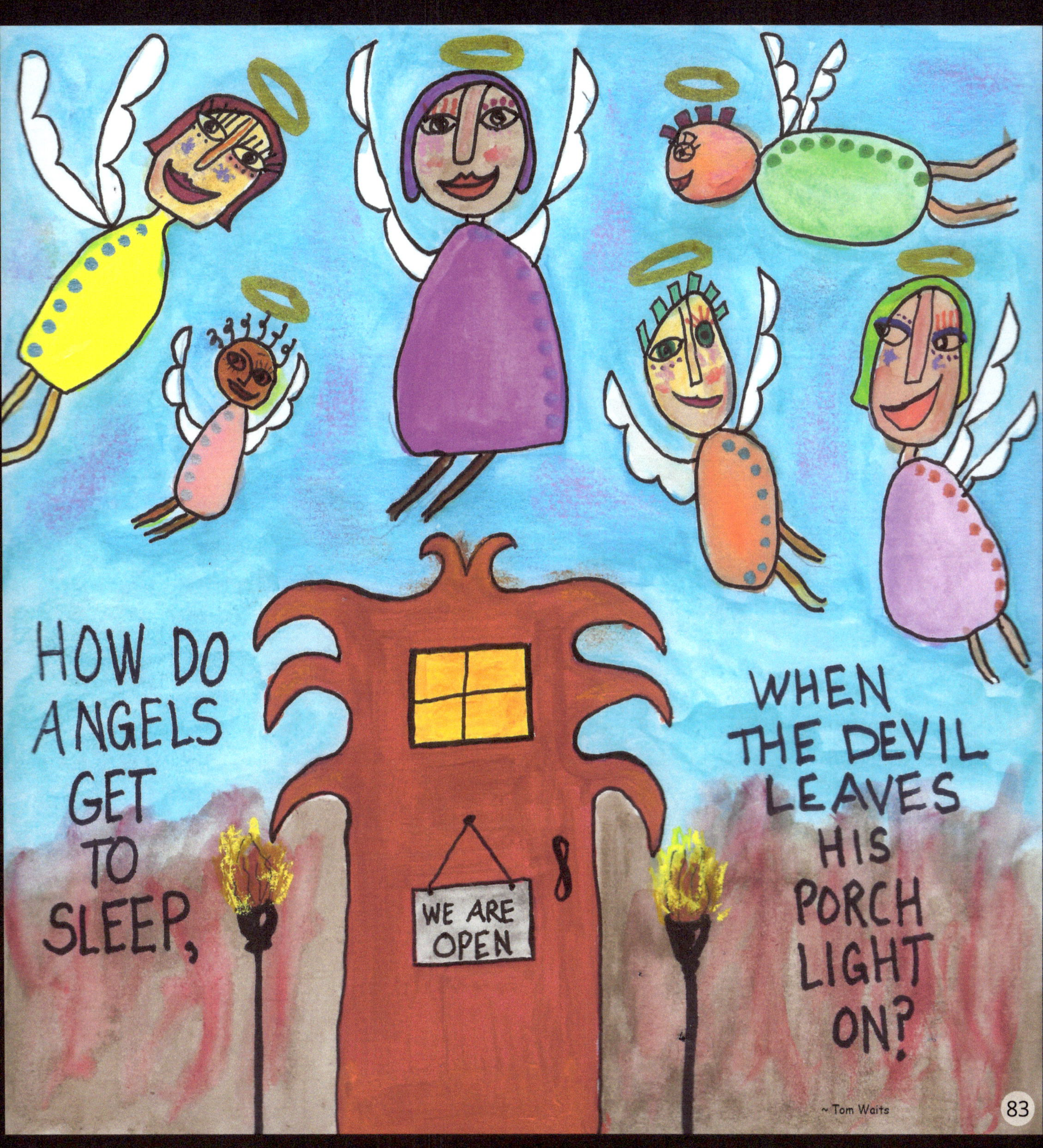
HOW DO
ANGELS
GET
TO
SLEEP,
WE ARE
OPEN
WHEN
THE DEVIL
LEAVES
HIS
PORCH
LIGHT
ON?
~ Tom Waits
83

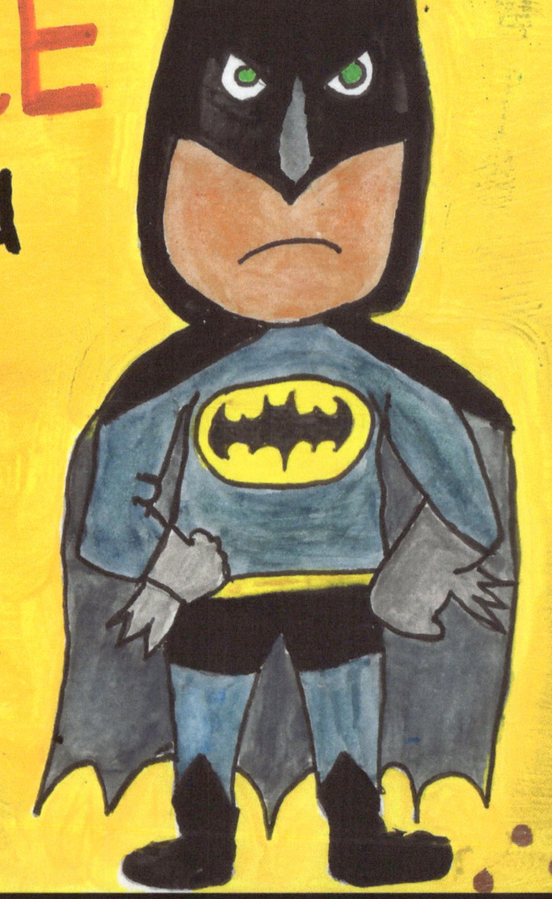

Whatever you're doing today, do it with the CONFIDENCE of a four-year old in a BATMAN COSTUME.

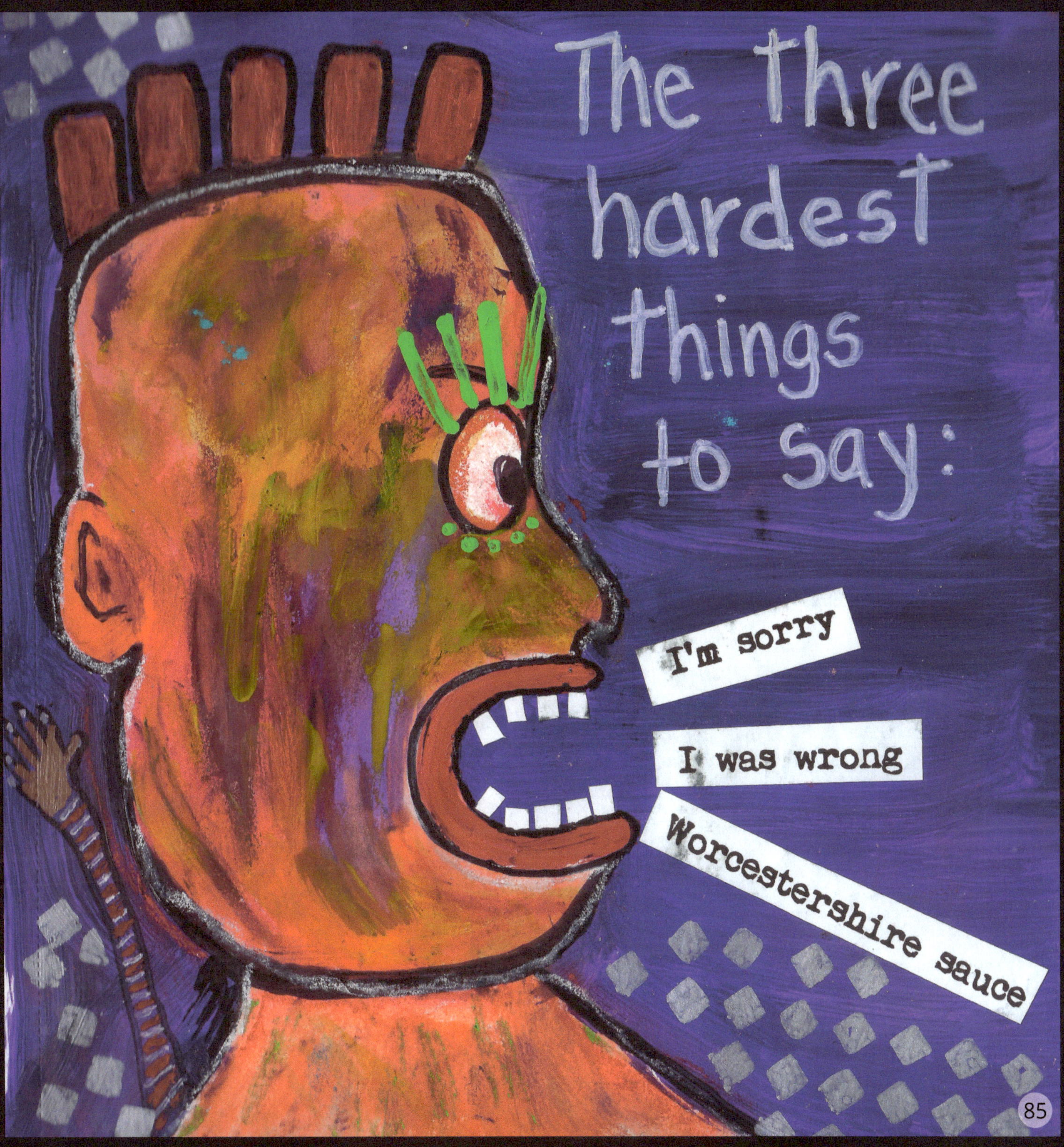

The three hardest things to say:
I'm sorry
I was wrong
Worcestershire sauce

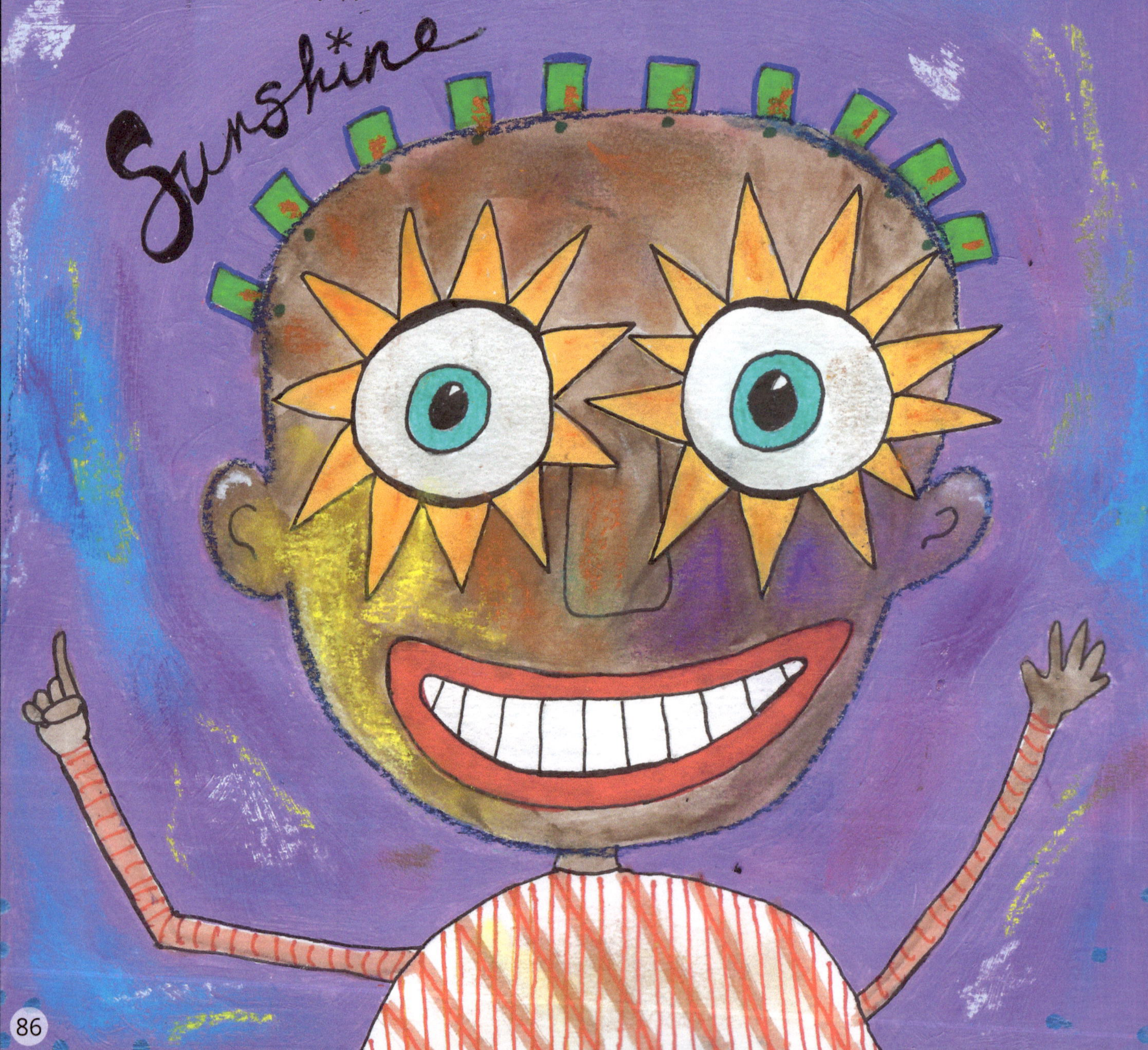

SOMETIMES
YOU HAVE TO CREATE YOUR OWN
Sunshine*

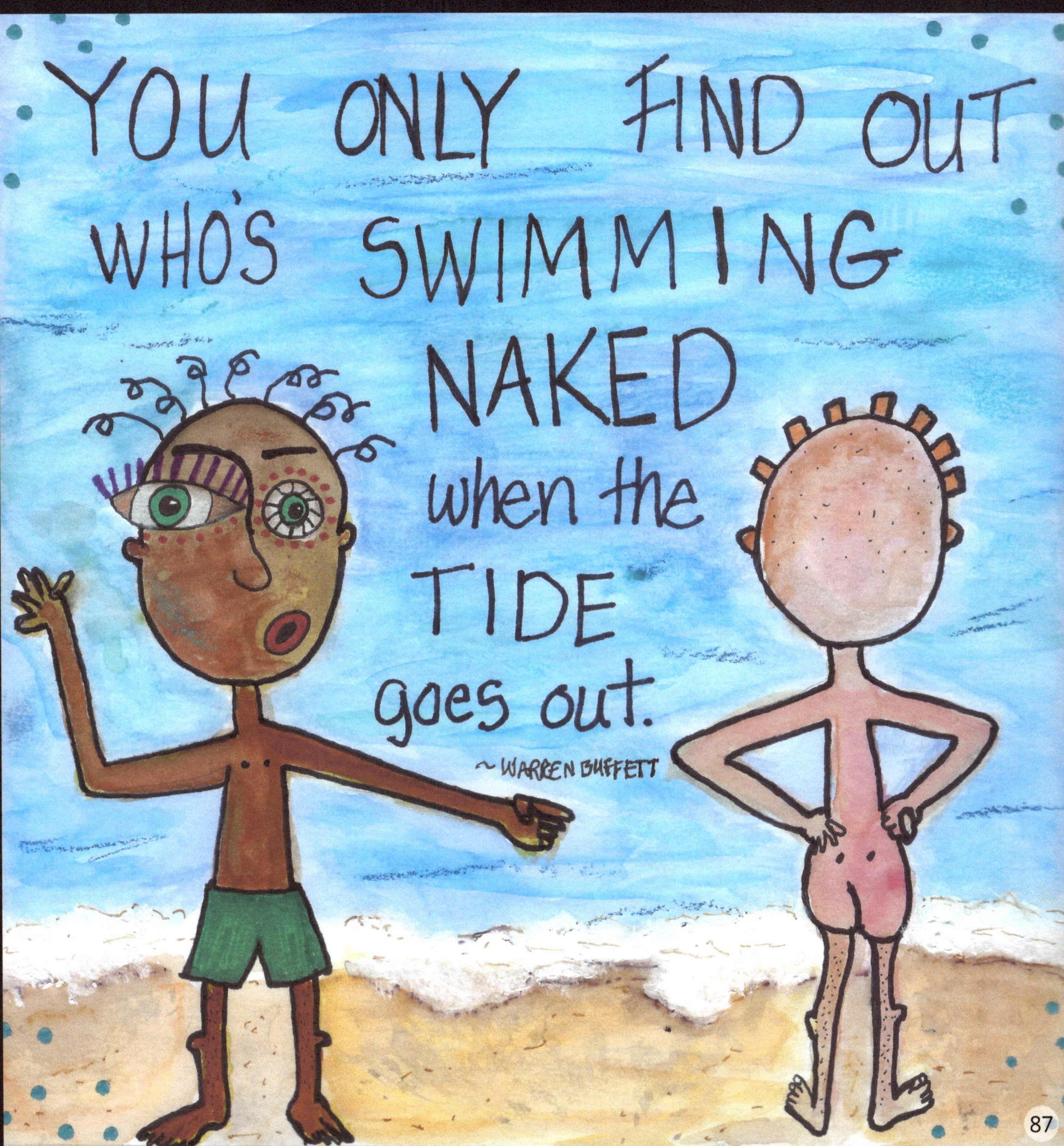

YOU ONLY FIND OUT WHO'S SWIMMING NAKED when the TIDE goes out.
~ WARREN BUFFETT
87

What
you plant
TODAY
You will
harvest
tomorrow

~Og Mandino

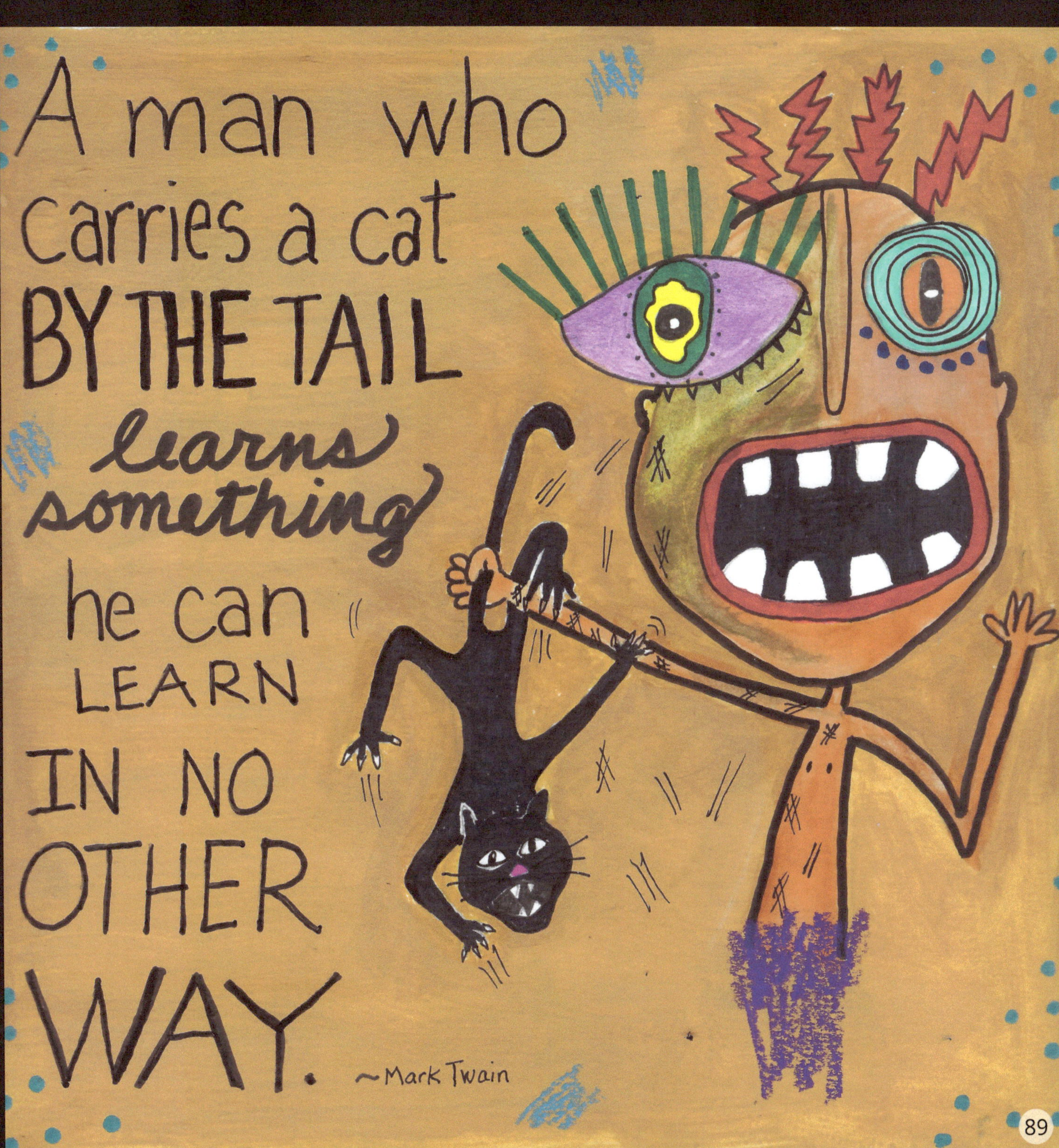

A man who carries a cat
BY THE TAIL
learns
something
he can
LEARN
IN NO
OTHER
WAY.
~Mark Twain

ONLY DEAD FISH GO WITH THE FLOW

~Andy Hunt

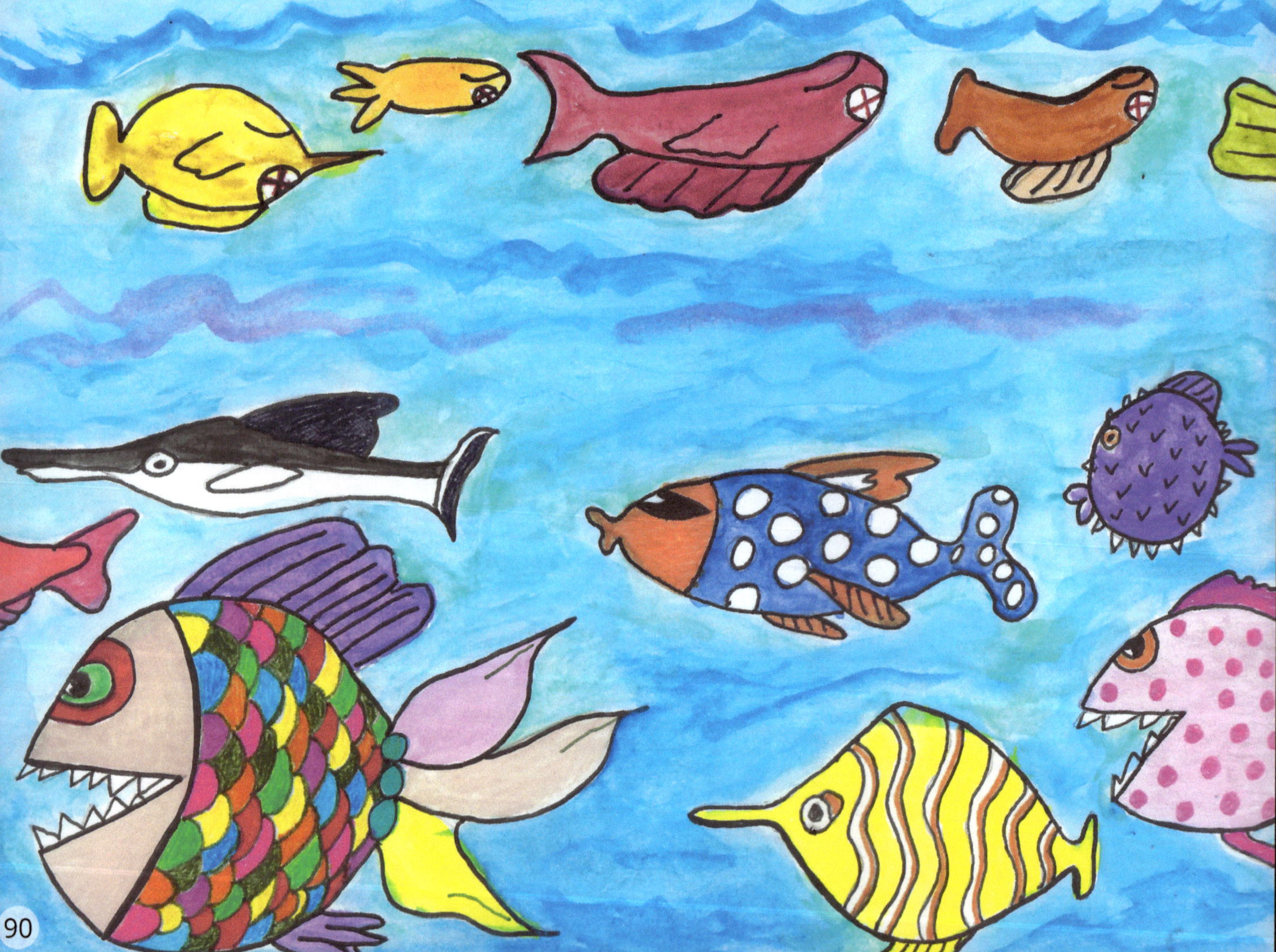

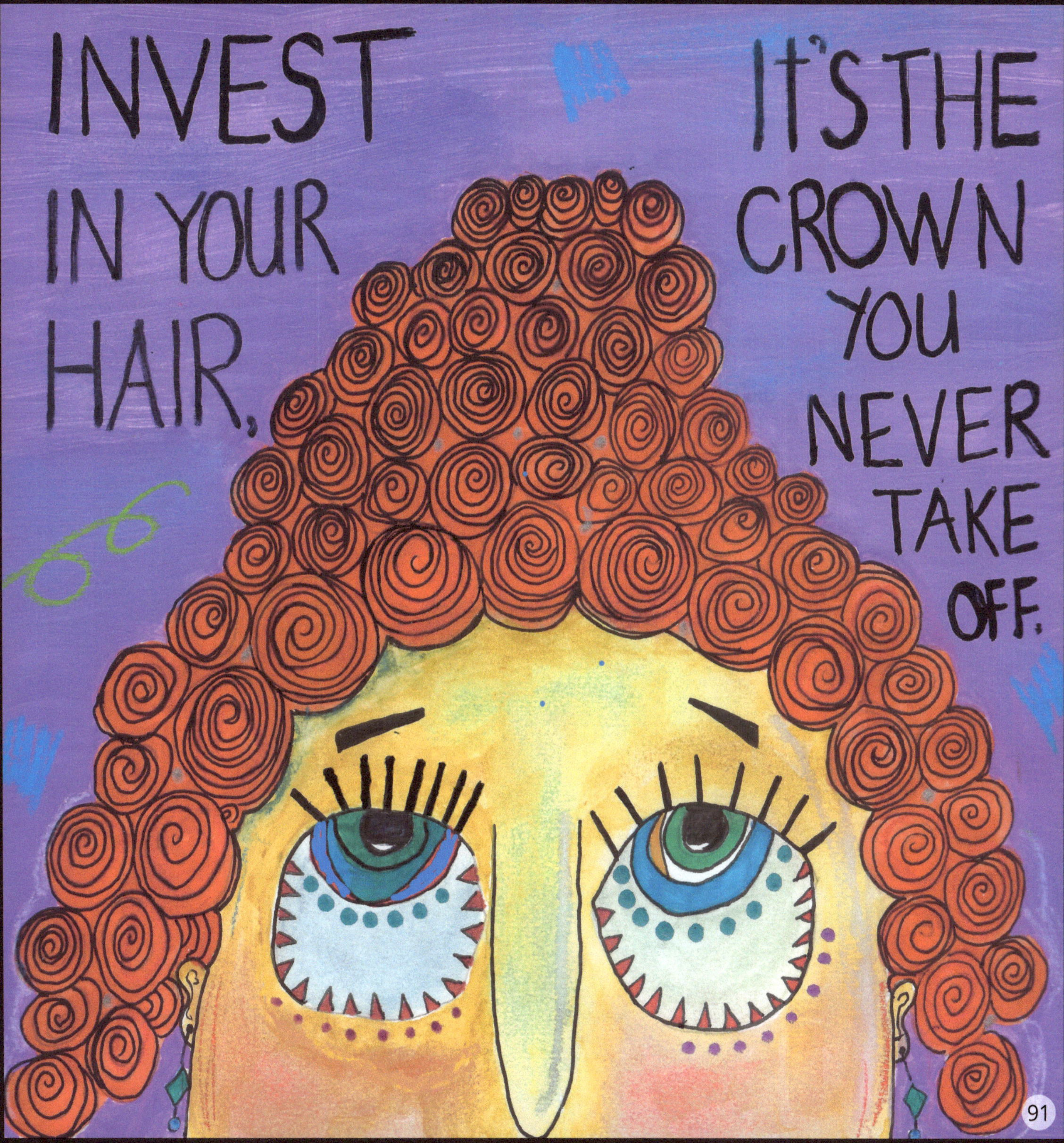

INVEST IN YOUR HAIR,
IT'S THE CROWN YOU NEVER TAKE OFF.
91

Early bird gets the worm, BUT it's the SECOND MOUSE that gets THE CHEESE. 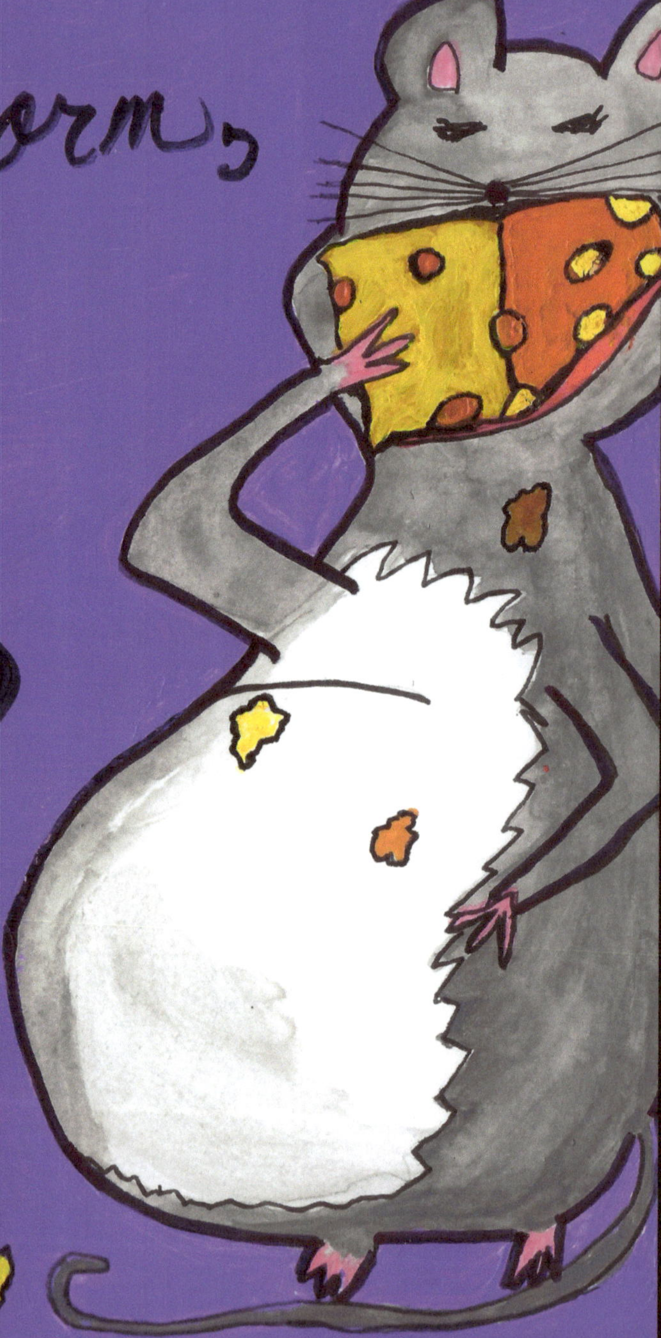
~ Willie Nelson

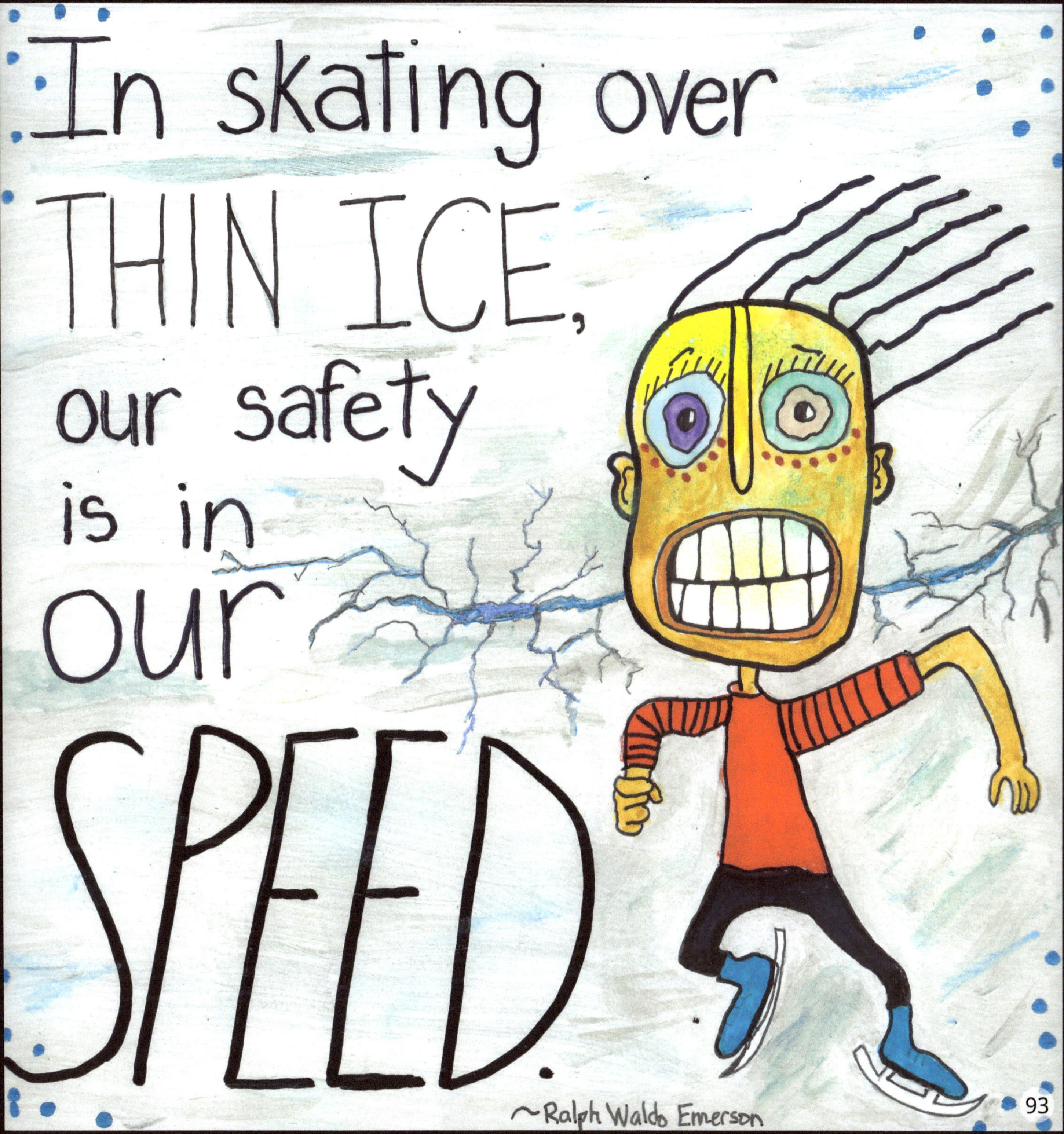

In skating over THIN ICE, our safety is in OUR SPEED.
~Ralph Waldo Emerson

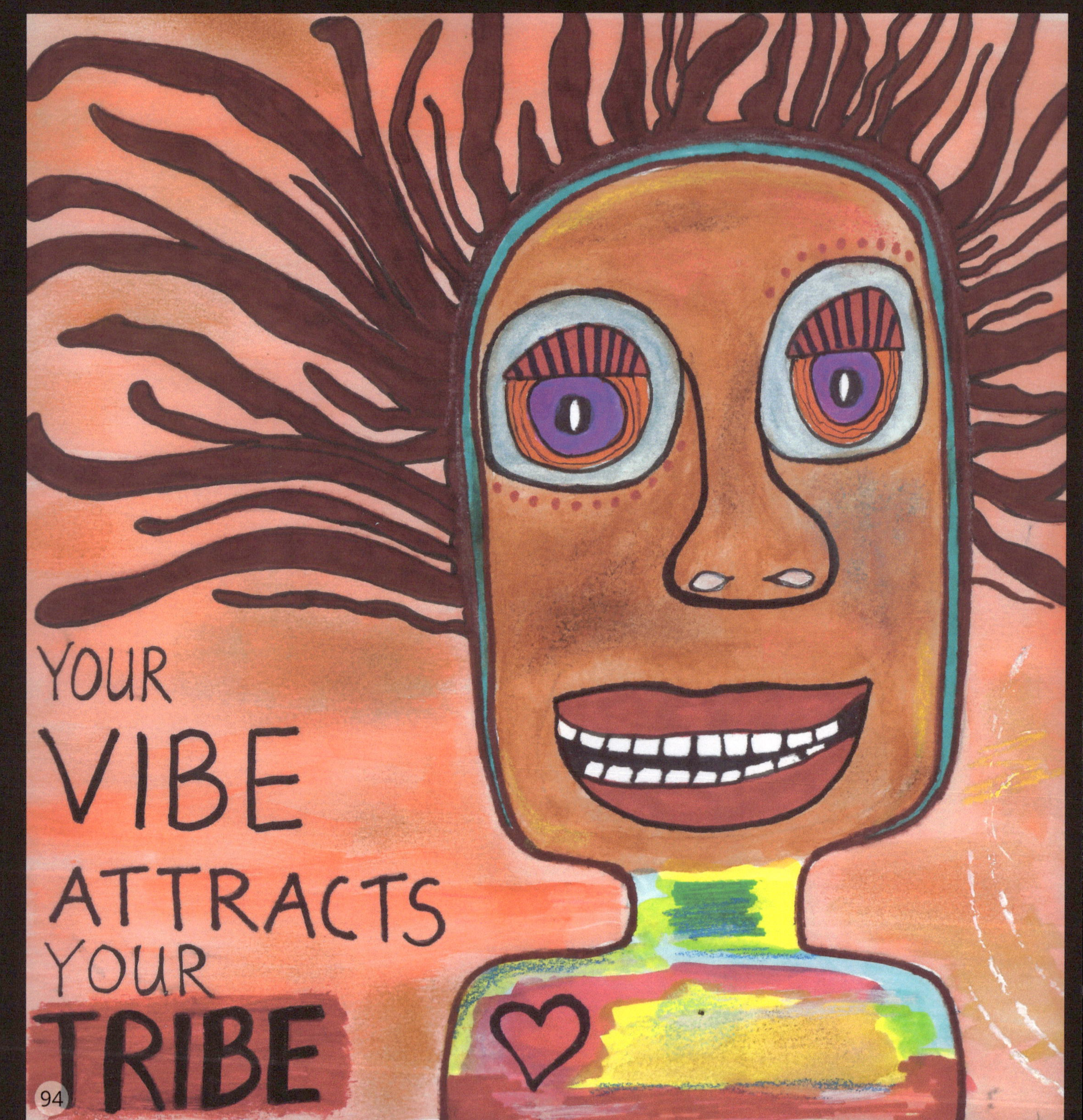
YOUR
VIBE
ATTRACTS
YOUR
TRIBE
94

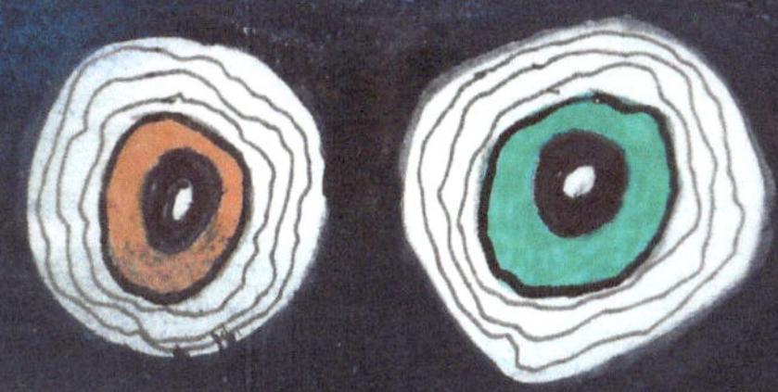

DON'T FORGET IN
THE DARKNESS
WHAT YOU LEARNED
IN THE
LIGHT
~ Joseph
Bayly
95

ART DISCUSSION QUESTIONS

1. Outsider Art is any work of art created by self-taught or untrained artists, or those outside of conventional norms of society. It usually has a naïve quality and is a personal expression created apart from any adherence to practices, styles, or trends in the art world. Is anyone previously familiar with Outsider Art?

2. Do you create art as a hobby, an amateur or professional?

3. When was the last time you tried to draw, paint, sculpt, or create an art project?

4. Have you ever sold any art? If so, what was the piece and where was it sold?

5. I went on a painting vacation in which a table and still life assortment was set up in the middle of a room. The instructor told us if we want our painting to look exactly like the display, we should get our cameras and take a photo. What we were painting was our impression of the display. That idea loosened me up to create more freely. Please share something that helped you move forward creatively.

QUOTE DISCUSSION QUESTIONS

1. Which of the Colorful Advice quotes is your favorite and why?

2. Have you ever laughed and had a beverage come out of your nose? Details, please.

3. How many of you have fried bacon in the nude? Would you do it again?

4. Tell us about a time you tried something new and sucked at it.

5. What is your idea of "adjusting your crown" before getting your day started?

6. Describe a stupid thing a friend asked you to do with them, and you did it.

7. Have you ever suffered the bad luck of the early worm?

8. Describe your "positive pants."

9. Tell about a time you proved stronger than your fears.

10. Tell us a good story about one of your bad decisions.

11. What have you planted today that you hope to harvest in the future?

12. Say aloud all together: Worchestershire sauce.

THANK YOU

"Silent gratitude isn't very much use to anyone."
~ Gertrude Stein

To my brother, David Hawkins, for his excellent artful eye and keeping me focused. He has been my biggest cheerleader on this project, critiquing every painting, sending LOLs late at night, and listening to the minutiae of the process.

To Cinnia Finfer, who provided canary-in-the-mine information about the self-publishing world.

To Hector Carosso, whose enthusiasm for the book gave me the needed backbone to move forward.

To Carla Green, who patiently answered a million questions, expertly turned 90+ paintings into a book, and helped keep me on track.

To all the friends and family who offered a favorite quote, a listening ear, and professional advice including Kim Cook, Deborah Parker, Barb Mende, Janet Appel, Don Bresina, Amy Lazenby, and Suzanne Riedel.

And finally, to Buddy, who insisted I get out of the art room and into some fresh air every day to play fetch with him.

INDEX BY QUOTATION

A bad attitude is like a flat tire. You can't go anywhere until you change it. 65

A man who carries a cat by the tail learns something he can learn in no other way. 89

Adjust your crown before getting your day started. 14

An apple a day will keep anyone away if thrown hard enough. 37

Bad decisions make good stories 71

Be brave enough to suck at something new. 7

Be careful when you follow the masses … sometimes the M is silent. 39

Be the person your dog thinks you are. 17

Be wary of having too little in your head, and too much in your tail. 42

Common sense is a flower that does not grow in everyone's garden 78

Count your age by friends, not years. 68

Discipline is choosing between what you want now and what you want most. 81

Do not corner something that is meaner than you. 41

Don't blame the clown for acting like a clown. Blame yourself for going to the circus. 66

Don't forget in the darkness what you learned in the light 95

Don't fry bacon in the nude. 5

Don't let anyone with bad eyebrows tell you anything about life. 77

Don't let yesterday take up too much of today. 72

Don't raise your voice. Improve your argument. 43

Don't spend time beating on a wall hoping to transform it into a door. 11

Don't sweat the petty things and don't pet the sweaty things. 53

Don't trade your authenticity for approval. 49

Early bird gets the worm, but it's the second mouse that gets the cheese. 92

Eighty percent of success is showing up. 46

Even if you are on the right track, you will get run over if you just sit there. 36

Everyone has a plan until they get punched in the face 30

Excellence is not being the best; it is doing your best. 48

Fall 7 times; stand up 8. 8

Five things you can control: words, attitude, manners, actions, effort 62

Flies don't enter a closed mouth 64

Friendship is like peeing in your pants. 58

Good friends don't let the friends do stupid things … alone. 38

Growing old isn't for sissies. AND It's not how old you are. It's how you are old. 32

Happiness often sneaks through a door you didn't know you left open. 61

Hate is a four letter word; so is love … 54

Holding onto anger is like drinking poison and expecting the other person to die. 35

How do angels get to sleep, when the devil keeps his porch light on? 83

Hustle + heart will set you apart. 44

I avoid looking forward or backward. Try to keep looking upward. 82

I've reached the age when, if someone tells me to wear socks, I don't have to. 52

If ifs and buts were candy and nuts, we'd have a party, wouldn't we? 40

If it involves fake smiling, don't go. 80

If you find yourself in a hole, the first thing to do is to stop digging. 6

In skating over thin ice, our safety is in our speed. 93

Invest in your hair, it's the crown you never take off. 91

It's what you learn after you know it all that counts. 33

Kind words can be short and easy to speak, but their echos are truly endlewss. 18

Laughter is a beautiful thing until milk comes out your nose. 3

Life begins at the end of your comfort zone. 76

Life is short. Smile while you still have teeth. 67

Live in such a way that you would not be ashamed to sell your parrot to the town gossip. 22

Live like someone left the gate open 56

Maintaining a positive attitude may not solve all your problems.
However, it will annoy enough people to make it worthwhile. 4

Make sure your worst enemy doesn't live between your own two ears. 51

Make your story so beautiful mermaids have trouble believing it's true. 73

May the bridge that you burn light the way. 45

Never slap a man who is chewing tobacco. 12

Never trust your fears. They don't know your strength. 63

No man has a good enough memory to be a successful liar. 16

One day or day one. You decide. 74

Only dead fish go with the flow. 90

Opportunity is missed by most people because it is dressed in overalls and looks like work. 10

Perhaps we consider too much the good luck of the early bird and
not enough the bad luck of the early worm. 57

Put on your positive pants! 19

Remember, if people talk behind your back, it only means you are two steps ahead. 15

Resist the devil and he will flee from you.. 26

Some talk to you in their free time and some free their time to talk to you. Learn the difference. 59

Sometimes you have to create your own sunshine.. 86

Speak your mind, but ride a fast horse. 27

Tact is the ability to tell someone to go to hell in such a way that they actually look forward to the trip. ... 24

Talking about bulls is not the same as facing them in the ring.. 47

The biggest troublemaker you'll probably ever have to deal with
      watches you from the mirror every morning.. 13

The devil's boots don't creak.. 20

The grass is always greener where you water it.. 31

The only person you should compare yourself to is the person you were yesterday. 23

The road of life is paved with flat squirrels who couldn't make a decision. 60

The three hardest things to say: I'm sorry; I was wrong; Worchestersire sauce. 85

There is no illusion greater than fear. 2

There is nothing so uncertain as a sure thing... 9

Wake up each day and tell the world to bring it. 79

We can complain rose bushes have thorns, or rejoice because thorn bushes have roses..................................... 34

Well, well, well, if it isn't the consequences of my own actions. 28

What you plant today you will harvest tomorrow. 88

Whatever you are, be a good one. 69

Whatever you're doing today, do it with the confidence of a four-year-old in a Batman costume. 84

When you come to a fork in the road, take it. 55

When you learn how much you're worth, you'll stop giving people discounts... 70

When you wallow with pigs expect to get dirty. 75

Wisdom is the reward for surviving our own stupidity. 1

Work until you no longer have to introduce yourself. 21

You can't stop the waves, but you can learn to surf... 29

You must at very least think noisy and colorfully, or you're not alive... 50

You only find out who's swimming naked when the tide goes out... 87

Your day will go the way the corners of your mouth turn... 25

Your vibe attracts your tribe... 94

INDEX BY AUTHOR

Abraham Lincoln 34, 69

Ain Eineziz... 38

Albert Einstein...................................... 52

Alisa Jacobs.. 44

Amy Morin 23

Andy Hunt... 90

Anonymous...............................39, 79, 91

Athena Singh... 63

Bette Davis | Jules Renard 32

Brian Rathbone 1

Charlotte Bronte.................................... 82

Coco Chanel 11

Cowboy Wisdom 41

Dan Nielsen... 66

Desmond Tutu 43

Dixie Willson 68

Ellis Vidler 71

Fannie Flagg 15

Franklin D. Roosevelt............................ 57

George Carlin 53

Harvey Specter, "Suits" 21

J.W. Stephens.. 17

James 4:7 26

Jet Li 59

John Barrymore..................................... 61

John Wooden 33

Jon Aculff 7

Jon Kabat-Zinn...................................... 29

Joseph Bayly 95

Justin Bieber.. 31

Karen Salmansohn 70

Laird Hamilton......................................51

Lao Tzu.. 2

Malachy McCourt.................................. 35

Mark Twain 89

Mel Brooks 50

Mike Tyson.. 30

Molly Ivins 6

Mother Teresa.. 18

Neal Donald Walsh 76

Og Mandino 88

Paulo Coelho... 74

Peggy Ward... 5

Phil Jackson 8

R.I.D. 73

Ralph Waldo Emerson 93

Robert Bloch... 58

Roy English 75

Scottish Proverb 20

Scotty Bowman....................................... 9

Spanish Proverb............................... 47, 64

Stephen Colbert 37

Texas Bix Bender................................... 27

Thomas Edison 10

Thomas Jefferson 16, 81

Tom Waits.. 83

Warren Buffett....................................... 87

Will Rogers........................... 12, 22, 36, 72

Willie Nelson 92

Winston Churchill 24, 25

Woody Allen 46

Yogi Berra.. 55

Zig Ziglar... 65